ALLEN BREED SERIES

The Allen Breed Series examines horse and pony breeds from all over the world, using a broad interpretation of what a breed is: whether created by the environment where it originally developed, or by man for a particular purpose, selected for its useful characteristics, or for its appearance, such as colour. It includes all members of the horse family, and breeds with closed or protected stud books as well as breeds and types still developing.

Each book in the Allen Breed Series examines the history and development of the breed, its characteristics and use, and its current position in Britain, together with an overview of the breed in America and worldwide. More difficult issues are also tackled, such as particular problems associated with the breed, and such controversies as the effect of the show ring on working breeds. The breed societies and their role in modern breeding policies are discussed.

BOOKS IN THE SERIES

The Arabian Horse

Sherifa, by Bahar ex Samiha, at the Royal Stud of Jordan.

ALLEN BREED SERIES

The Arabian Horse

Rosemary Archer

J. A. Allen
London

British Library Cataloguing in Publication Data

Archer, Rosemary
  The Arabian horse.
  I. Title
  636.112

ISBN 0–85131–549–6

Published in Great Britain in 1992 by
J. A. Allen & Company Limited
1 Lower Grosvenor Place, London SW1W 0EL

Series editor Elizabeth O'Beirne-Ranelagh
Book production Bill Ireson
Printed in Great Britain by The Bath Press, Avon

Contents

Front cover: Sherifa, the Hamdanieh Simrieh mare purchased by the Blunts in 1878 and ridden by Lady Anne Blunt on their travels through the desert, pictured here with her 1880 foal, Shehrezade, a filly by Kars. Painting by Stephen Pearce, private collection. Photograph Roger Bastable.

Front endpaper: Parade of Arabian horses at Crabbet Park.

Back endpaper: The scene at a typical start in Arab racing, Goodwood, 1985.

Acknowledgements

The author would like to thank Betty Finke, Michael Bowling, Charmaine Grobbelaar, Joan Flynn and the Earl of Lytton for their kind assistance and for providing photographs. Also the Arab Horse Society for provision of archival material. Especial thanks to Diana Dykes for many hours spent helping to prepare the manuscript.

   Thanks also to the following for the use of their photographs: John Elliott, Janet Harber, Wills Keevil, Trevor Meeks, Photonews, Judith Ratcliff, Peter and Marilyn Sweet, Rik van Lent, and to Jill Pezare for her line drawing.

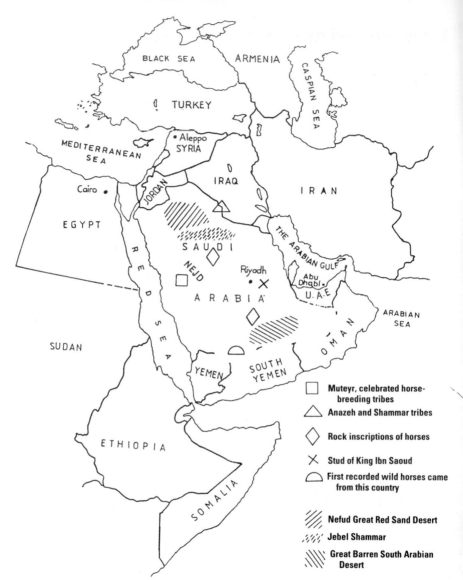

The Arabian peninsula and surrounding countries, showing important areas for Arab breeding according to Lady Wentworth.

1 Origin and history of the breed

The Arabian is the oldest pure breed of horse in existence. It is regarded as the root stock of all southern hot-blooded horses, as compared to the northern cold-blooded type from which evolved the heavy breeds.

Antique sculpture and the many rock drawings depicting horses of Arabian appearance found in the Yemen date back to 600 BC. The Chaldeans are said to have had Arab horses before 1000 BC, and there are many references to horses in Syria being captured in wars and taken to Egypt around that period; horses appearing on Egyptian wall inscriptions show distinct Arabian type with small head, arched neck and high tail carriage. It is probable that the Arab horse has existed in the Arabian peninsula, which includes modern Iraq and Syria, for at least 3,000 years.

The exact origin of the Arabian has always been a controversial subject amongst writers and authorities who have put forward a number of theories. It will probably remain a mystery since the antiquity of the breed makes it unlikely that conclusive scientific source evidence can ever be forthcoming. One theory is that the Arab horse stemmed from the borders of Siberia; another that it originated in Libya. Wilfrid and Lady Anne Blunt and their daughter, Judith, Lady Wentworth, believed that it was a separate breed native to the Arabian peninsula. Wilfrid Blunt was interested in the importance scientists attached to the distinctive tear-gland site in the skull of the Arabian and the set-on of the tail.

Lady Anne Blunt is renowned as one of the greatest authorities on the Arab horse. A brilliant scholar, she was fluent in Arabic and spent much of the later part of her life in her Egyptian home where she studied the works of early Arab writers and poets; she also had close contact with the horse-breeding tribes of Arabia. The Blunts had travelled extensively in North Africa and the Arabian peninsula and were well-known amongst the Bedouin. Lady Anne's detailed journals of their travels and her knowledge of the Arab horse gained through direct contact with Arabs provide some of the most important information we have on the breed and its history.

Lady Anne reached the conclusion that there were two distinct classes of opinion concerning the horses of Arabia. She called the first the voice of tradition (Nejd and Inner East) and the second the voice of romantic fable (Islam and the outer East). The first she further described as the 'Nomad' voice of Nejd, which had its own original local tradition that the horse existed in ancient times in a wild state. The second she said might be called the 'Islamic' voice which had adopted the original tradition of the first but 'grafted on it a fantastic fable of romantic legends'. She explains that in the truly Nomadic tribes a certain independence of mind inherited from pre-Islamic times had never died out. These opinions are important for they help in differentiating between the genuine traditions of the Bedouin, and the 'myths' originating in the misapprehensions of some writers.

The pre-Islamic tradition of a wild horse in Arabia is supported by the fact that the peninsula was once fertile and well watered, but that for some thousands of years it had been slowly drying up. One traditional tale is of a wild horse first tamed by Ishmail, the son of Abraham, around 1400 BC. King Solomon, in about 950 BC, is said to have possessed a stud of 1,000 Arab horses.

Probably the earliest written mention of horses in the Arabian peninsula is in the Book of Job. Many legends from the first few centuries AD, passed down by word of mouth from generation to generation and later put into verse by post-Islamic poets, concerned the Arabs and their horses. Europeans who have travelled amongst the tribes speak of children playing the game of 'wild horses'. Lady Anne Blunt stressed the significance of the strong belief held by the Bedouin in the descent of their horses from a wild breed, and their pride in its ancient lineage.

The Bedouin and their horses

From its earliest mention the Arabian horse has been admired for its beauty and noble bearing, but the desert is no breeding-ground for weaklings. Both man and beast had to endure extremes of climate, scarcity of food and a rigorous way of life: only the fittest could survive. Although the Arabs treasured their mares they expected them to bear the same privations as their owners, and their lot was a hard one.

In the days of constant tribal warfare when *ghazus*, or raids, were a common occurrence, the lean and often half-starved mares would carry their masters for countless miles across the desert at the gallop, for the Arab often had to rely on the speed and endurance of his horse for his very life. Only when a mare had a young foal was she left at the camp; at all other times she would be ridden on forays and this would continue until she was old and too weak to take part any more.

News travelled fast in the desert and little went on that did not become generally known amongst the tribes.The breeding of their horses was as well known as the

Ibn Saoud's stud at Sulaimiya (Kharj) in 1934.

marriages of their people and equally well guarded, there being a fanaticism amongst the Bedouin to keep their horses' blood pure and not tainted by crossing with *kadishes*, animals of inferior antecedents.

Nejd, in the interior of Arabia, is accepted to have been the centre of the great Arab horse-breeding tribes. Amongst those known to have bred the best horses are the Roala, Muteyr, Khatan, Shammar and Anazeh. Constant migrations north-wards in search of pasture for the summer months kept the tribes continually on the move and some became more settled in areas outside central Arabia, but still continued to breed *mazbut* (pure) horses.

Since stallions would be likely to betray the presence of raiders by neighing when approaching an enemy camp, they were never used in *ghazus*. Only colts destined for breeding were retained by the Bedouin. The Arabs consider gelding a disgrace and brutality, and inferior unwanted colts were sold to village dealers or townspeople, who fattened them up and sold them elsewhere.

3

The mares were sometimes kept tethered with woollen hobbles in the Bedouin camps, but often ran loose; those with foals might be looked after by the women. In times of war mares might be shackled with iron chains and padlocked against theft by an enemy. If a party was on a *ghazu* its members would usually, if the enemy was at a distance, make the journey on camels and lead the war mares, who would then be fresh for the foray.

Amongst a number of superstitious beliefs held by the Arabs was the fear that a new foal would be endangered if it was gazed upon by 'the evil eye' (that of someone who might be coveting the animal, or turn out to be an enemy) and so precautions had to be taken to prevent any stranger seeing it. This belief also applied to important new acquisitions and in such cases there would be a ritual of sacrificing a lamb, and smearing its blood on the forehead of the horse for good luck. Lady Anne Blunt described seeing a newly born foal which had hung round its neck on a string a tar-soaked ball of wool done up in a rag of cotton, believed to be a 'smelling-bottle' capable of warding off any evil to the foal.

The horses' rations were often meagre and consisted mainly of dry herbage, supplemented with dates and camels' milk, and sometimes barley, but the migration of the tribes each spring provided fresh pasture and then the horses would be turned loose to graze. Water was strictly rationed and horses were only allowed to drink at regular intervals in camp, or from any springs or pools found on their travels. Foals were weaned at three or four months old and further reared on camels' milk given in a wooden bowl. After weaning they were tied to a tent-post at night, a collar around the neck, but when the tribe was on the march they followed loose. Young children would often scramble on to the backs of yearlings, which having been reared in close proximity to humans were usually very tame. Europeans on first seeing Arab horses in Bedouin camps invariably remarked on their quiet disposition, shown by the manner in which the mares when loose would wander into their master's tent for attention, or when inclined would use a human as a rubbing post.

At two years old breaking began with a *reshmeh* (head-collar) only. Later they would be ridden with a small saddle-pad without stirrups. The true Bedouin rode their horses with a *reshmeh* but townspeople would often use a bridle and bit formed from a ring of iron encircling the lower jaw and thus acting as both bit and curb-chain. They would be taught to circle and complete figures of eight. Lady Anne Blunt comments that one lesson in particular was good exercise for teacher as well as horse: the rider would tie the *reshmeh* to his hand and then repeatedly throw

4

himself off. At first the horse would try to get away, dragging the rider, but in time it learnt to stand immediately he fell. In this way it became accustomed to its rider falling, so that if he should come off in a fight it would stand still waiting for him to remount.

The training the Bedouin gave to their mares had the sole object of teaching them to respond to the needs of mounted fighting and the pursuit of enemies.

2 Early collections of Arabians

The beauty and scarcity of the very best Arabian horses have, over the centuries, led those with power and wealth to acquire collections of them.

El Naseri

One of the earliest recorded collections is that of the Egyptian Sultan El Naseri (AD 1290–1342), whose vast importations to Egypt were carefully set down in a contemporary history compiled for the Sultan's library. He is reputed to have paid enormous sums of money for the best specimens from the horse-breeding tribes of the Nejd, and from Bahrain, Hasa, Katif and Iraq.

Lady Anne Blunt noted some records from El Naseri's Stud Book. Numerous horses are mentioned for their prowess as well as for their beauty and nobility. Racing was already popular in the Middle East and it seems that the Sultan was particularly fond of the sport. In addition to praise for their great speed in races, horses were written of which had jumped wide rivers, one being said to have cleared 40 feet of water!

The Amiri Stud of Bahrain

The ruling family of Bahrain, the Al-Khalifa, are descended from a great Anazeh tribe and claim Al-Haeear, in southern Nejd, as their ancestral home. At the end of the seventeenth century, divisions within the tribe resulted in the Al-Khalifa migrating to the east coast of Arabia and the Gulf region. After further divisions within the family and ensuing battles amongst the clans and against neighbours, Sheikh Ahmed captured the island of Bahrain and became its first Al-Khalifa ruler.

In traditional Bedouin manner the Al-Khalifas built up a collection of Arabians, often acquiring mares from tribal sheikhs who used the island as a sanctuary at times of mainland warfare.

Sheikh Ahmed died around 1796 and was succeeded by his sons, Sulman I and Abdulla, who established the Kehileh Jellabieh strain in the stud. History relates that the original mare, who was bred and owned by Sheikh Jarshan of the Utaiba tribe, was celebrated in the desert for her speed and courage in war, and when

A 22-year-old mare of the Krush strain at the Amiri Stud of Bahrain in 1969.

Abdulla heard this he sent word that he would like to have her. It transpired that Sheikh Jarshan had recently been killed in battle and his riderless mare captured by Jellab, of the Al-Murra tribe. Jellab would not at first part with such a famous mare but was persuaded to sell a half share to Abdulla and she went to Bahrain. When she produced a filly foal Jellab claimed the mare back as his share but Abdulla did not want to let her go; eventually Jellab accepted in her place 10,000 gold rials and the filly, so the mare remained in Bahrain and went on to found a family which today is still considered one of the most precious in the stud.

Sheikh Sulman's grandson, Mohammed, was one of the most colourful characters of the nineteenth century, but he only ruled for a very short time, in between wars with his uncle and later his brother. He was a contemporary of Abbas Pasha (see below) and sent many horses to Egypt, some of which left descendants which appear in the pedigrees of present-day Arabians.

In 1903 Isa ibn Khalifa, grandson of Sulman I, presented a bay mare of the renowned Dahmeh Shahwanieh strain to Abbas Pasha II, Khedive of Egypt, and four years later this mare, named Bint el Bahreyn, was purchased by Lady Anne Blunt for her Sheykh Obeyd Stud outside Cairo. There she produced two fillies and from the second, Dalal, there descends a large family which has been influential in Arab horse breeding throughout the world.

More recently other Amiri mares have also founded important families outside Arabia, notably Nuhra who was imported into England.

Feysul ibn Saoud

In the 1860s the centre of power in Nejd was with Feysul ibn Saoud. W. G. Palgrave, writing of his journeys in Arabia at that time, described a visit to the stud at Riyadh. He was immensely impressed with the horses, saying that they surpassed anything that he had seen, or even imagined he might find in Arabia. The prevailing colour of the horses was chestnut and grey, and he wrote of them as being quite small, but so exquisitely shaped that their size was no defect. He maintained that with their intelligent and yet singularly gentle look and an air and step which commanded admiration they fully justified their reputation as the finest collection in the desert.

Mohammed ibn Rashid

The leadership of central Arabia passed to Emir Mohammed ibn Rashid at Hā'il and the Blunts visited his stud in January 1879. By then Feysul's stud had diminished to only a fraction of its size and former glory, but some of the horses had passed to Ibn Rashid's predecessors and at the time of the Blunts' visit his stud was considered to be the best in Nejd.

The Blunts, however, were disappointed at first; the horses were at their worst, unkempt in their winter coats and herded in open yards in the town. They nevertheless noted their beautiful heads and later, when witnessing a spectacular display outside the city walls when Ibn Rashid and about 50 riders took part in a sham fight, Lady Anne described the horses as becoming transfigured when mounted and in motion.

Arab rulers frequently presented each other with gifts (often in return for help received in wars or political struggles) and these were commonly in the form of horses. Ibn Rashid presented 29 Arabians to the Sultan at Istanbul in 1889; four years later Wilfrid Blunt visited his stud and remarked that the best horses there were those which had come from Ibn Rashid.

The Abbas Pasha collection

The most important collection of Arabians made before the twentieth century was that of Abbas Pasha I, Viceroy of Egypt from 1848 to 1854. Many modern Arabians are descended from his horses and some carry 50 per cent or more of this blood.

The stud was founded by Abbas Pasha's grandfather, Mohammed Ali, who was appointed Viceroy of Egypt in 1805. In the course of various campaigns in Arabia Mohammed Ali acquired a magnificent collection of Arabians, many being captured from Riyadh and other oasis towns. The horses, however, were said to have been very poorly looked after by their Egyptian grooms and many died from illness and neglect, cooped up in small yards and badly fed. But still they remained an extremely valuable collection.

During this time the young Abbas Pasha developed a passion for the breed which was to lead to the establishment of his world-famous stud. Abbas Pasha became friendly with Prince Feysul ibn Saoud and when the latter was imprisoned in the citadel of Cairo in 1842 (probably on account of a dispute over the payment of tribute) it is said that he planned the escape of the Prince. The friendship enabled Abbas Pasha to purchase a large number of horses of the best blood-lines to be found in Arabia; indeed he bought up all that were available of one of the finest strains, the Seglawi Jedrans of Ibn Sudan. He gave large prices for many of the horses, £7,000 being quoted as the figure for a mare of the Jellabieh strain. One elderly mare, unable to travel the long distance from Hā'il to Cairo, was considered so precious that she was said to have been conveyed to Egypt on wheels.

Having begun his own collection during the lifetime of his grandfather, Abbas Pasha then acquired all he could from the stud of Mohammed Ali, who had died in 1848, and continued to buy more horses through his agents who scoured north Arabia for even more valuable mares and stallions.

At the time when the Abbas collection was at the height of its glory there are believed to have been close to 1,000 horses which were kept at various places in Egypt. Abbas Pasha spent a vast amount of money building an enormous palace of pink and white marble in the desert at Dar el Beyda, between Cairo and Suez, with magnificent stables and a huge underground cistern providing water for stone troughs from which the mares drank. Then in 1854 Abbas was assassinated and the palace at Dar el Beyda and the horses passed to his son, El Hami Pasha. However, he had little chance to enjoy his inheritance for having been invited to Constantinople he was made to marry into the Sultan's family and was detained there.

Miserable at being kept away from Egypt and the stud, he fell into the hands of financial adventurers who eventually robbed him of enormous sums. Before long he was forced to sell about half the stud but it seems no record was kept of where the horses went.

When El Hami died in 1860 his affairs were found to be in such a bad state that to satisfy the claims of creditors auction sales of the remainder of the stud took place.

At these sales a few horses were purchased by Europeans, principally from Italy and Germany, the envoy of the King of Württemberg being one buyer, but a son of the Governor of Syria, Ali Pasha Sherif, was able to purchase a large number. With these precious remnants of the great Abbas collection he built up a stud in Cairo which at its greatest in the 1870s numbered some 400 horses. Then a horse plague, alleged to have been introduced by the troops of Ishmael Pasha returning from Abyssinia, struck the stud and the epidemic wiped out many valuable strains.

Ten years later Ali Pasha Sherif still had over 100 horses, but as his personal circumstances deteriorated, so did the stud and on his death in 1897 the remnants were sold, fortunately to dedicated breeders.

Abbas Pasha had ensured that full records of his horses were kept and these stud books, together with those of Ali Pasha Sherif, formed an invaluable history of the original desert-bred mares and stallions. When living in Egypt Lady Anne Blunt obtained permission to see these treasured books and it is largely through her notes that so much information is available on the world-famous stud. The gradual dispersion of most of the collection was looked upon as a calamity for Arab horse breeding by Lady Anne, for by the end of the nineteenth century high-class Arabians were becoming scarce in the desert. However, the saving of the remnants by her and a few other single-minded breeders ensured that the Abbas Pasha blood was not lost altogether.

The Blunts and Crabbet

Lady Wentworth remarked on her father's ability always to collect around him objects of beauty; with their interest in horses it is hardly surprising that Wilfrid and Lady Anne Blunt became collectors of Arabian horses. They went to Aleppo in Syria in 1877, originally intending to seek out a horse of the same strain as the Darley Arabian; but under the enthusiastic influence of J. H. Skene, the British Consul, they conceived the much bolder plan of collecting mares and stallions of the best Anazeh blood, taking them back to England and breeding from them at Crabbet Park, their home in Sussex.

Although at that time some European studs were breeding a few purebred Arabians, the horses procured in Arabia and brought to Europe in the past had largely been used to improve local stock. The Blunts planned to build up a stud of pure Arabians, believing that a source of the best blood available outside the desert would be of great value: at that time they also thought it possible that a fresh infusion of Arab blood into the Thoroughbred might prove beneficial to that breed, although in fact this was never attempted. Skene had travelled extensively and had acquired considerable knowledge of the Bedouin and their horses and he told them that high quality Arabians were becoming more and more difficult to find in the desert.

Thus the Blunts began searching for the best horses and their first purchase was made on 25 December 1877 when they bought a bay yearling filly of the Kehileh Dajanieh strain. They named her Dajania and she became one of their most important foundation mares.

Skene was well acquainted with the sheikhs in the area around Aleppo and the journey into the desert was planned with his help. Mounted on their own horses and accompanied by a few servants with camels, the Blunts spent three months travelling amongst the tribes, ending their journey in Damascus. They visited a number of Bedouin camps and made friends with some of the most important sheikhs. In addition to buying for their stud they both became so enchanted with the desert, the Arabs and their horses, that a whole new epoch began in their lives, which was to have a resounding consequence on Arab horse breeding throughout the world.

The Blunts made two more journeys to the Arabian peninsula and in 1881 purchased more horses; they imported 29 desert-bred mares and stallions into England. No group of Arabians was selected more carefully. Lady Anne was indefatigable in searching out the background of each horse and only those of undoubted *mazbut* breeding were considered suitable as foundation stock. Individually chosen for their quality and general conformation, any horse which failed to produce foals of a high standard was subsequently culled. In addition both mares and stallions were ridden or driven in harness, therefore soundness and temperament were fully tested and any showing signs of weakness or defect were eliminated from the stud. Meticulous records of the horses were kept by Lady Anne and, together with photographs dating from 1882, form a unique source of information on the Crabbet Stud.

In addition to Dajania, the most important foundation mares included the chestnut Rodania, a Kehileh Rodanieh who was a celebrated mare in the desert, the bay Abeyeh Sherrakieh Queen of Sheba, another famous mare purchased only after protracted negotiations lasting several months, and also Basilisk, a grey Seglawieh Jedranieh of Ibn ed Derri, and Ferida, a bay Managhieh of the strain of Ibn Sbeyel.

The first imported stallion used at Crabbet was Kars, who had been ridden by a Kurdish chief to the war in Armenia in 1877 and had a miraculous escape although twice hit by rifle fire. On the retreat from Armenia to Aleppo, Kars appeared so exhausted that his saddle and bridle were taken off and he was left behind, but he got up again and followed his master. Both reached Aleppo in a state of collapse and Kars was still hardly out of danger when seen and purchased by the Blunts. When fully recovered he became Wilfrid Blunt's favourite mount and was hunted for several seasons.

The Crabbet Stud soon became well known as a source of pure blood and consequently there was much demand for colts and stallions from overseas countries, mostly for upgrading local horses. Wilfrid Blunt was never able to resist good offers for Crabbet horses and this resulted in some of the finest, such as Azrek, a magnificent grey Seglawi Jedran of the famous Ibn ed Derri strain who was purchased in the desert and imported in 1888, and Hadban, a bay Hadban Enzeyhi of the Oteybeh tribe, bought in India by the Blunts in 1883, being sold before a male line had been firmly established at Crabbet; though valuable through their daughters, their early departure from the stud was always regretted by Lady Anne. Kars and Hadban went to Australia where Kars left some purebred descendants, whilst Azrek was sold to South Africa and his line was lost.

In 1882 the Blunts bought a property outside Cairo, Sheykh Obeyd Garden, named after a saint who, according to local tradition, had been one of the Prophet's

The bay Hadban Enzeyhi of the Oteybeh tribe, bought in 1883 and imported by the Blunts in 1884 when six years old. Hadban was the sire of two of the most important Crabbet mares, Rose of Sharon out of Rodania, and Nefisa out of Dajania.

companions and whose tomb stood in the grounds; it consisted of 37 acres of rich soil which in the 1830s had been planted with fruit trees. They rebuilt the main house and spent the winter months of each year there.

When at Sheykh Obeyd the Blunts used to visit Ali Pasha Sherif's stud in Cairo and in the winter of 1888–9 they made their first purchase from the Pasha, a filly and two colts, one of which, a chestnut Seglawi Jedran of Ibn Sudan's strain named Mesaoud, became one of the most influential stallions ever. Mesaoud proved to be a remarkably successful sire when crossed with the Blunts' desert-bred mares; their progeny went to countries all over the world and today his name appears many times over in pedigrees.

In 1891 the Blunts purchased Sobha, a beautiful white Hamdanieh Simrieh mare whose famous sire, Wazir, was bred by Ali Pasha Sherif from Abbas Pasha stock

13

The great Mesaoud (1887) by Aziz ex Yemameh, the first and most important stallion the Blunts purchased from Ali Pasha Sherif. A Seglawi Jedran of Ibn Sudan's strain, Mesaoud had a world-wide influence on Arab horse breeding.

and whose dam, Selma, was Abbas Pasha's original mare of the strain. Imported into England in 1891 her female line is still flourishing in Britain and in several other countries around the world.

More horses of Ali Pasha Sherif blood-lines were bought by the Blunts when they became available and so, with those purchased at the final auction of the remnants of his stud, they became the owners of over 30 horses of this breeding. The best were sent back to England and the remainder formed the Sheykh Obeyd Stud which continued up to the time of Lady Anne's death in 1917, when it was sold and the horses dispersed amongst breeders in Egypt.

The blend of desert-bred Arabians and those imported later of Abbas Pasha blood-lines produced excellent results, not surprisingly since the horses had all originated from the same desert sources. The Crabbet Arabian stud prospered and in addition to colts and stallions sold abroad for up-grading, mares and stallions were exported as foundation stock for pure breeding – in fact, Crabbet-bred horses formed almost the whole of the early foundations of Arab horse breeding in Australia and South Africa and accounted for a large proportion of that in the USA. Today there is hardly an Arab horse stud book in the world which does not list horses with Crabbet blood in their veins.

The 'Pink House' built by the Blunts at Sheykh Obeyd Garden. After their separation in 1906, Lady Anne spent many winters here.

Important Crabbet horses

Amongst the important early horses bred by the Blunts mention should be made of Ahmar (Azrek ex Queen of Sheba). Although sold when comparatively young and leaving no sons at Crabbet, his four daughters, Selma and Siwa (out of Sobha) and Bukra and Bereyda (out of Basilisk's daughter Bozra (by Pharoah)), all founded notable families whose descendants are now spread around the world.

Before his exportation to Australia Hadban sired two very important daughters, Nefisa, out of Dajania, and Rose of Sharon from Rodania. Nefisa was a prolific brood mare, producing in all 21 foals, the last at the age of 27. Her two most significant daughters were Narghileh (by Mesaoud) and Nasra (by Mesaoud's son Daoud), she being the dam amongst others of the stallions Naseem and Naziri (both by Skowronek) and the mares Nezma, Nisreen and Nashisha. Nefisa's numerous descendants include notable horses such as Nizzam (who went to Holland and then on to the USA), Blue Domino, Champurrado, Indian Gold, Indian Magic, Sindh (in Australia) and Serafix (USA), and a host of other stallions which have made a great contribution to the breed. In fact her line is exceptional for the many top-class sires it has produced.

Rose of Sharon, whose golden chestnut colour with flaxen mane and tail and white markings is still prevalent in her descendants, produced Ridaa by Merzuk. Merzuk was one of the Blunts' Ali Pasha Sherif imports, whose quick sale abroad (to Basutoland) was afterwards regretted, for he had only one season at Crabbet. Ridaa had three important daughters, Risala by Mesaoud, and Riyala and Rim, both by Astraled (Mesaoud ex Queen of Sheba), another remarkable stallion. Risala, foaled in 1900, a particularly fine mare, produced the stallion Rasim (by the Ali Pasha Sherif horse, Feysul) and the mares Rafina (exported to Australia), Rythma and the great Rissla, by Berk, a son of Bukra. Rissla combined the beauty, quality and style which are so striking in her family with the brilliant action of her sire, inherited from Ahmar. Rissla's foals include Rifala who with her son Raffles went to the USA where they became famous; Reyna, sold to the Duke of Veragua in Spain, and who became important in early Spanish Arab horse breeding; Rissalma, who with her daughter Florencia went to Russia in the batch sold by Lady Wentworth in 1936, and there produced the extremely important stallion Priboj; and Risslina, through whom the Rissla female line is most strongly represented in Britain today. Rissla's best-known son, Rissalix by Faris, left strong male lines which include such horses as Count Dorsaz (exported to the USA), Blue

Domino and Mikeno, whilst her son Irex, famed for his exceptionally beautiful head, features in the pedigrees of many of today's show winners.

Of the Ali Pasha Sherif mares imported by the Blunts Sobha proved by far the most important, mainly through her daughters Selma and Siwa. Selma's main daughter Selima (by Astraled) was the dam of the stallion Shareer and of Star of the Hills, another who went to Russia where her line became established and proved very important in the Tersk Stud, and Sotamm (by Astraled) who was exported to Egypt with his son Kazmeen, bred at Crabbet from Kasima. Kazmeen became one of the Egyptian Royal Agricultural Stud's most influential stallions.

Indian Magic (1944) by Raktha ex Indian Crown, held by Fred Rice at Roehampton in 1957 when he was Male Champion.

Rissla (1917) by Berk ex Risala, in front of the tennis court at Crabbet. One of the most famous Crabbet mares, she produced a large family whose influence spread throughout the world.

Siwa was the dam of Somra, whose daughter Safarjal was a foundation mare of H. V. M. Clark's Courthouse Stud in England, and of Silver Fire, one of the most beautiful mares at Crabbet, of whom it has been said she founded a dynasty in her own right. Her finest daughter, Silver Gilt, by the great sire of brood mares, Indian Gold, was the dam of Silver Vanity. Silver Fire's descendants are prominent in Australia and the USA as well as in England.

In 1906 the Blunts separated. He remained at Newbuildings Place, his house near Horsham, and Lady Anne spent the winters at Sheykh Obeyd and the summer months at a rented house near Crabbet. The stud was partitioned between them with half the horses established at Newbuildings and half at Crabbet. Following Lady Anne's death there was a complicated legal dispute between Blunt and his daughter which went in favour of Lady Wentworth, and in 1920 all the horses were reunited at Crabbet. Lady Wentworth was a brilliant breeder and under her guidance the stud entered into the period of its finest glory.

An important addition, in fact the first outcross in 40 years, was the stallion Skowronek. Through the early sale of Azrek, Shahwan, Seyal and others, there were no grey stallions in the stud when it came into the hands of Lady Wentworth, despite the fact that Lady Anne Blunt had for many years been trying to procure a suitable animal from Arabia. Skowronek was bred by Count Potocki at Antoniny, a Polish stud which the Blunts had visited many years before, and was by an original importation to Poland, Ibrahim, out of a mare from one of the long established female lines of the Antoniny Stud. Owned at the time by Mrs H. V. M. Clark, Skowronek was seen at a show in March 1920 by Lady Wentworth and shortly afterwards he was installed at Crabbet. He proved to be a highly successful sire with the Crabbet mares and re-introduced the grey colour into the sire lines of the stud. His most famous son was Naseem, out of Nasra, who through his sale to the USSR in 1936 was to have a profound influence on Arabian breeding in that country and in Poland, and later the USA.

It is not possible in this short survey of the Crabbet Stud to mention more than a few of the important horses directly descended from the Blunt imports, but suffice it to say that no other privately owned stud has influenced Arab horse breeding on a world-wide scale over so long a period. The stud continued to prosper for the rest of Lady Wentworth's life and when she died in 1957 it was inherited by her former manager, Cecil Covey. Death duties forced him to sell many horses and 15 years later he disbanded the stud when a motorway was built across Crabbet Park. The remnants were all sold within a few days of announcing their availability, and all

During the 1950s Lady Wentworth held annual parades at Crabbet to which friends, breeders and other groups were invited. Lady Wentworth stands with stud groom Fred Branch, admiring Indian Magic. On the left, with her back to the camera, is Miss May Lyon.

21

Naufal (1916), by Sotamm out of Narghileh, in a parade of horses at Crabbet for King Fuad. (Note the smartly dressed groom with polished shoes and cap held under his arm.)

Lady Wentworth with Skowronek at Richmond Royal Show in 1924.

went to British breeders, some of whom continued to breed solely from the Crabbet blood-lines.

Since that time Arabians bred in other countries descended from desert root-stock have been universally popular but in the last few years there has been a clear revival of interest in horses of Crabbet breeding. Shows and other events specifically for Arabians of these blood-lines are run by Crabbet Groups in Australia and the USA and are becoming increasingly prestigious.

3 British studs

Arab horses had been imported into Britain for centuries, but always with the aim of improving existing stock rather than for pure breeding. Initially they were popular for racing and, according to Lady Wentworth, in the fourth century there were covered training hippodromes at five centres in Britain in which Arab horses were raced. She writes that the first racehorses recorded by name are Arundel, an imported Arabian stallion owned by Sir Bevys of Hamptown, and Truncefice, an Arabian mare of Bradmond, King of Damascus, which raced at the court of King Edgar in London in 957, Truncefice winning. Countless numbers of Oriental horses were imported in the seventeenth and eighteenth centuries, including a large number of mares collected at great expense by Charles II and which became known as the 'Royal mares'.

The Crabbet Stud was the first to import significant numbers of mares and stallions for pure breeding, and a number of other studs during the same period were influential on the future of Arab breeding in Britain.

The Hon. Miss E. Dillon's stud

A contemporary of the Blunts, the Hon. Miss Ethelred Dillon, was an effusive admirer of Arab horses. She believed that the Arabian had the strength, soundness and overall good qualities to be considered the best horse for general purposes, and she went to all lengths to prove it. Tireless in promoting the breed, she donated prizes at shows and wrote unceasingly to numerous newspapers and periodicals singing its praises. Miss Dillon bred crossbreds as well as purebreds and she practised what she preached, sometimes even to excess when driving her horses too hard.

She founded her stud in Oxfordshire with a few Crabbet mares which she bred to her own imported stallions and during the latter part of the nineteenth century hers was the only other stud of any consequence in England. One of her most notable purchases was Hagar, Wilfrid Blunt's journey mare who had carried him so well on the desert travels.

Miss Dillon's stud, however, is probably most influential through the progeny of her stallion El Emir, which she bought in Algiers and imported to England in 1880. She became devoted to the horse and took him with her everywhere, even to India where she spent the winter three years later. El Emir worked as hard for his living as all the others, being one of her principal driving horses as well as being ridden, and he displayed tremendous powers of endurance.

Miss Dillon's other important stallion was Maidan, who came to England via India and was purchased by her in 1889. Well known for his racing prowess in India, Maidan was by then 21 years old but still did a season's hunting in Suffolk and even won a steeplechase.

In addition to the two stallions Miss Dillon acquired an imported mare, Ishtar, and it is through her foals by El Emir that the stud is most strongly represented today. Ishtar's son Imam (who at one time was an officer's charger in South Africa) sired Imamzada who was exported to the USA where his daughter Rosa Rugosa was very influential in the early days of Arab horse breeding in that country. Another of Imamzada's daughters, El Lahr, went to Australia in 1901 and founded a large family through her daughter Al Caswa.

Imamzada's dam, Kesia II, was out of a Kehileh Nowagieh mare named Kesia. She was imported, a few years before the Blunts began their search for horses, by Captain Roger Upton, who made a journey to Arabia to purchase horses for Henry Chapman, MP and also the Australians W. J. and A. A. Dangar. The Kesia line still exists through her granddaughter Ruth Kesia, whose sire was a son of Azrek.

Boanerges, a full-brother to Imam, was the great grandsire of Shahzada, the winner of long distance tests of 300 miles in the early 1920s in England before his exportation to Australia.

During the 1880s Miss Dillon's financial problems caused her to offer her horses for sale on numerous occasions, but she always retained a few until in 1898 a final auction sale at Chipping Norton effectively marked the end of the stud. Miss Dillon died in 1910.

The Courthouse Stud

From the mid 1920s up to 1957, three studs dominated the Arab horse scene in Britain: Crabbet, Hanstead, which belonged to Lady Yule and her daughter Gladys, and Courthouse, owned by Mr and Mrs H. V. Musgrave Clark.

At the age of 19 Henry Vyvyan Musgrave Clark went to the USA to spend two years on cattle ranches in Texas and New Mexico. There he lived and worked with the ranchers and met such rough and tough customers as Pat Garrett who killed the celebrated outlaw, Billy the Kid.

On his return to England Clark studied estate management and in 1910 he bought the Crabbet stallion Mansur. His dedication to the breed had been fired by a dark chestnut Arab stallion, Bashom, seen at Saffron Walden market; Clark had been filled with admiration for the horse on learning how he had reputedly cantered non-stop for 50 miles with vital despatches before the battle of Omdurman in 1898. After collapsing from exhaustion Bashom had been rolled in a pit and covered with banana leaves by Sudanese troops, but had made a complete recovery by the next morning.

The most famous horse Clark owned was Skowronek, who was imported into England in 1913 by Walter Winans, an American sculptor. During the First World War he passed into the hands of Mr Webb-Ware who later sold him to Clark. Skowronek had been used on only a very few mares before Lady Wentworth saw him in 1920. Clark initially quoted her a very high price, but she finally managed to acquire the stallion via an agent.

By the early 1920s Clark had acquired several Crabbet mares, including Belka, by Rijm out of Bereyda. He rode Belka to victory in the 300 mile endurance test of 1921 and she afterwards proved a fine brood mare, leaving many descendants including Belkis II, Benjamin and Bahram, the last two being champion stallions at the British National Show.

'Bill' Clark and his wife, Audrey, finally settled at Courthouse Farm, under the South Downs in Sussex, and with the arrival from Crabbet of Safarjal, a gift from Lady Wentworth to Mrs Clark, their stud flourished. Safarjal, by Berk out of Somra, came in foal to Rasmin and the bay colt she produced, Sainfoin, became the stud's most important stallion. He was a wonderful show horse, winning the stallion championship at the Arab Horse Society's London show seven times between 1927 and 1936; and completing a 'double' by also winning the ridden class in 1931, 1932 and 1936. In addition he won a 1½ mile race in 1929.

The second stallion of importance at Courthouse was Champurrado, by Irex out of Niseyra and of Crabbet blood-lines but bred by Lady Yule. He was purchased to perpetuate the type of Arabian Clark preferred, comparatively small with a lovely head and good overall conformation. Bill Clark's declared preference for the smaller Arabian was to lead him into a direct conflict with Lady Wentworth which erupted into letters from both to the press. Clark wanted the Arab Horse Society (AHS) to bring in a ruling that no Arabian should be registered in the Society's stud book if over 15 hands in height; Lady Wentworth strongly objected, saying that the Arabian was a horse, not a pony, and such a height limit was ridiculous. The AHS

Bahram (1946) by Sainfoin out of Betina. A typical Courthouse stallion, he was Male Champion at the AHS Show, Roehampton, in 1954.

firmly rejected Clark's proposal but the argument between the two forceful breeders rumbled on for some years. Despite their disagreement, Lady Wentworth respected Clark's judgement, but he would only consent to judge at one show – the Royal Agricultural Show – at which he once made two Crabbet horses Champion and Reserve!

In its heyday Courthouse was a force to be reckoned with in the show ring and the horses included such fine winners as Shammar, Somra (not to be confused with the Crabbet Somra) and Sherifa, as well as the 'B' line descendants of Belka; her daughter Bekr was by Nimr, one of the three imported stallions used at Courthouse, the others being Fedaan and Atesh. Mr Clark did not breed many foals each year, and stallions tended to be well into maturity before beginning stud careers, so that some only sired two or three foals in a lifetime. In addition outside mares were rarely accepted at stud, and since the foals bred were highly priced and overseas buyers favoured, British breeders had little chance to acquire Courthouse stock. However, later in his life Clark did allow his stallions to be used more often, and this together with the sale after his death in 1981 of some of his mares enabled breeders to obtain more Courthouse blood.

The Hanstead Stud

In July 1925, a visit to Crabbet was arranged for a lady, ostensibly a breeder of Anglo-Arabs. The visitor turned out to be the wife of multi-millionaire Sir David Yule, and Lady Wentworth afterwards admitted that she had foolishly sold Razina to her for an inadequate figure. In view of Lady Yule's professed interest in Anglo-Arabs the offer of Razina was an obvious one since Lady Wentworth had recently re-purchased her from Mrs Carroll in Ireland and she had come over in foal to the Thoroughbred Mighty Power.

Sir David Yule had built up a huge fortune in India and he and his wife and daughter, Gladys, lived at Hanstead House, a magnificent estate in Hertfordshire. Lady Yule and her daughter were both keenly interested in farming and they bred Jersey and Aberdeen Angus cattle and Suffolk Punch horses.

Razina, who was by Rasim out of Riyala, duly produced the filly Razzia by Mighty Power. Visitors to Hanstead in pre-war days got the impression that Lady Yule seemed more interested in her Anglo-Arabs than in purebreds, and also in the Thoroughbreds which she raced very successfully. However, she was an astute breeder and realising that she had a very good foundation mare in Razina thereafter she was bred only to Arabian stallions.

Sir David Yule died in 1928 and Lady Yule is reputed to have announced that she intended to enjoy spending his fortune, said to have been £30 million. Land was bought back in, twenty new stables were erected and a yacht, named *The Narlin* – after the first Thoroughbred to win for her on the turf – was built for half a million pounds; her maiden voyage was a dawn to dusk cruise for all the estate workers.

Lady Yule and her daughter were both very kind and were always helpful,

Twenty-first birthday party for Grey Owl (1934) by Raseem ex Naxina. Miss Gladys Yule cutting the 'cake' with Miss Pat Wolf standing behind and the stud groom, Sam Simmonds, holding Grey Owl, at Hamstead House.

particularly to young or new breeders. They both also shared a genuine concern for the welfare of animals and it was typical of their practical approach to make available premises at Newmarket for the Animal Health Trust and jointly to donate money to the Trust and other deserving causes.

In 1930 Razina produced her most famous daughter, Nurschida, by Mr Hough's stallion Nuri Sherif. She was the dam, amongst others, of Sulka, who left a strong female line through Queen Zenobia, whose sire Radi was Razina's first foal bred in

29

Ireland by Mrs Carroll (Radi later went to Crabbet and then to Hanstead), and Namilla, dam of Mikeno and Count Manilla, who had a notable show ring and sire record in Australia. Namilla left descendants in South Africa too, where her daughter Correze made a great impact as a foundation mare of the Jamani Stud.

In 1932 Mr and Mrs Kent, who were well known in pony breeding circles, expressed a wish to see the mares at Crabbet, and during their visit asked if they could buy two. This was agreed and they chose Astrella and Naxina; within a week both were at Hanstead. No doubt Lady Wentworth understood the predicament of well known or wealthy buyers in England, for she found that whenever she herself became interested in a horse the price was put up, as had been the case with Skowronek. Lady Wentworth had a keen sense of humour and probably considered Lady Yule's tactics as all part of the game. In any event the affair seems to have drawn the two breeders together for thereafter the Hanstead mares were sent to Crabbet stallions, starting an interchange of stock which proved of great benefit to both studs.

Two years later Razina produced her most famous son, Raktha by Naseem. As a youngster he was acquired by Lady Wentworth and was for many years one of the leading sires at Crabbet before being exported to South Africa at the age of 16. Raktha's progeny included such stallions as Indian Magic, Serafix (a leading sire of champions in the USA), Electric Silver who went to Australia, and the mares Grey Royal, a great show-winner in England, and the lovely Silverlet who was exported to South Africa.

Razina's next foal was Riffal, by Naufal, a very tall horse who stood nearly 16 h.h. He finally went to Australia and became one of the most influential sires there. His son Oran, out of Astrella and bred at Hanstead, was another who made his name at Crabbet. The exchange of stock worked both ways as during the war Rissalix went from Crabbet to Hanstead and was the leading sire there for many years. Astrella was a great-granddaughter of Queen of Sheba and it is through her that a female line of this family still exists.

Naxina's best-known son was Naseel, a small beautifully proportioned grey, closely bred to Skowronek. Naseel was purchased by Mrs Nicholson in Ireland and his fame as a sire of partbreds is described later. Naxina also produced two important daughters in Samsie, by Riffal, and Naxindra by Indian Gold.

Just before the war Lady Yule acquired the last of the four Crabbet-bred mares which formed the basis of her stud. This was the exquisite dark chestnut Niseyra, by Rissam out of Neraida. In addition to producing Champurrado, she was the dam of

Blue Domino (by Rissalix), who sired a legion of top-quality horses including Ludo, Manto, Blue Magic, Domatella, Blue Rhapsody and the full sisters Dreaming Gold and Golden Treasure. Stock from Blue Domino was exported all over the world and the unmistakable quality of this prepotent horse is clearly noticeable in his descendants.

Later in the war the relationship between Lady Wentworth and Lady Yule became somewhat strained, which was hardly surprising since both were strong-minded independent personalities. Lady Wentworth believed that the main cause of the break which occurred between the two studs was her refusal to sell Lady Yule the magnificent colt Indian Grey, by Raktha out of Indian Crown, a full brother to Indian Magic. Lady Wentworth considered him exceptional and not even Lady Yule's high offer tempted her to sell him. Thwarted in her endeavours to buy Indian Grey, Lady Yule then refused to sell Oran when Lady Wentworth wanted to buy him in 1943. A year later she did sell Oran to Mr C. McConnell, who then sold him on to the British Bloodstock Agency from whom Lady Wentworth bought him. This appears to have been the final straw for Lady Yule and resulted in a complete break in their relationship.

In 1946 Lady Yule handed over her entire stud to her daughter, but she still continued to attend the Arab Horse Society shows which were then held in the lovely grounds of Roehampton, on the edge of London. Four years later she died.

Gladys Yule was a very popular figure in equine circles. She was the Chairman of the Ponies of Britain Club and did much to assist the preservation of native breeds, as well as encouraging the inclusion of Arab blood to produce fine riding ponies and horses. She was especially interested in the ridden Arabian, and her Count Dorsaz (Rissalix ex Shamnar, a daughter of Razina) twice won the Winston Churchill Cup for the Supreme Riding Horse at the Royal International Horse Show. It was a memorable sight to watch the beautifully schooled chestnut stallion give his spectacular display at the White City, when as a finale he would race at high speed round the arena and then stop dead in his tracks in a couple of strides, to tremendous applause!

Miss Yule added one more important mare to the Hanstead Stud, Rafeena by Mr Hough's Aluf out of the Crabbet Ranya II. She had already produced Rikham who was exported to Australia and became an important sire there. At Hanstead she had Iridos, Count Rapello and Grantchester, who was another to go to the Jamani Stud in South Africa, where he was their leading sire. Hanstead was not only a keen rival of Crabbet in the show ring, but also very important for the Arabians it

One of the Hanstead-bred horses acquired by Lady Wentworth for Crabbet, Oran (1940) by Riffal out of Astrella, an important sire.

exported. It was interesting to compare the horses of Crabbet, Hanstead and Courthouse in the show ring. Mr Musgrave Clark, with his preference for small Arabians, was producing animals which came to be acknowledged as the 'Clark type'. Many people referred to a 'Hanstead type' which, though perhaps lacking the exceptional presence and style that was a hallmark of the Crabbet Arabians, could equal them for quality and action.

When Lady Wentworth died in the summer of 1957 Gladys Yule's comment was

Count Dorsaz (1945) by Rissalix ex Shamnar by Naziri. Bred at Hanstead, he won the Ridden Class at the Royal International Show four times and the Winston Churchill Cup for Supreme Riding Horse on two occasions. Later he was exported to the USA to be a leading stallion at Mrs Bazy Tankersley's Al-Marah Arabians.

'now we can go back to Crabbet'. But sadly this was not to be, for a few weeks later she herself died. And so came the end of a great era in Arab horse breeding in England.

Miss Pat Wolf, a close friend of Miss Yule, was left options on the Hanstead horses but, as in the case of Lady Wentworth's estate, most of the horses had to be sold to pay death duties. Some went to British owners and Blue Domino lived on for nine more years available to British breeders. The Hanstead Stud had existed for only 32 years but its influence as a British stud was widespread and only surpassed by Crabbet itself.

The Harwood Stud

Harwood has the distinction of being the oldest stud in England today. It was founded in 1896 when Colonel Lyon bought the mare Howa, who was by Azrek out of Hagar's granddaughter Harra, at the Crabbet sale of that year.

The Lyons lived at Horsham and would sometimes ride out to nearby Newbuildings Place when the Blunts were living there. Lady Anne recalled one occasion when Colonel Lyon, his son, and his daughter May, who was riding Howa, told her that they had been trying Howa's speed against the son's hunting mare, who was said to be very fast, but Howa beat her. The Hagar line through Howa became established at Harwood and when Colonel Lyon died his daughter carried on the stud, later adding other mares of Crabbet breeding, including Rosalina, Naxindra and Yavroum.

May Lyon was a very keen breeder of Arabians, and she greatly admired Lady Anne Blunt and was a staunch supporter of Lady Wentworth. An unmistakable figure at Arab Horse Society shows and events, she held forthright views which she was never reluctant to air. For many years Miss Lyon ran two studs, having moved some of the horses to Rostrevor in Ireland where her brother lived. On her death in 1962 her property was inherited by cousins, Mr and Mrs R. H. Calvert and their daughter Georgina (Mrs J. Moore). The horses from Ireland were brought back to Sussex and under the Calverts' capable management the Harwood Stud has flourished.

George Ruxton

George Ruxton bought Maisuna, by Mesaoud out of Meshura, from Crabbet in 1907, and then the stallion Nadir, and he bred from them at his Craven Lodge Stud near Basingstoke. Maisuna was also hunted for three seasons and regularly driven.

Mr Ruxton had strong ideas on the type of Arabian he admired most and he later acquired the very good stallion Algol, who had been bred by the Prince of Wales (later Edward VIII) and was by a son of the imported Dwarka out of the Crabbet mare Rangha.

Algol proved an important sire and from his daughter Myola Mr Ruxton bred

G. Ruxton's well-known stallion Algol (1928) by Aldebaran out of Rangha, bred by the Prince of Wales (King Edward VIII). Algol won numerous prizes under saddle as well as in-hand and in 1933 was Champion Male at the London Show.

Dargee. Lady Wentworth bought Dargee as a yearling and he won many championships in the post-war Crabbet era, and sired some fine stock.

Sydney Hough

Before the First World War Sydney G. Hough was breeding polo ponies and hunters at his home in Essex when he commenced using Arab stallions on his mares. Impressed by the resulting foals he decided to breed pure Arabians, so he bought Nureddin II (Rijm ex Narghileh) from Wilfrid Blunt, and Shahzada, who was bred by H. C. Stephens, and the mares Ruth Kesia and Amida.

Mr Hough was one of the founders of the Arab Horse Society. He has been described as a daring and reckless rider and driver of horses; Lady Wentworth once recounted a terrifying drive with him whilst being rushed to catch a train after visiting his stud. Sydney Hough was killed out hunting in 1923 and his son Cecil continued the stud and bought in more mares. One of Cecil Hough's best known stallions was Shihab by Algol out of Amida's daughter, Almas.

William Hay

William Hay started his stud at Winestead Hall in Yorkshire just before the Second World War and his principal stallion was Rish's son Rangoon, by Skowronek. Mr Hay acquired the Crabbet mare Somara, a daughter of Silver Fire by Nureddin II, and produced a string of fillies from her by Rangoon, including Silver Crystal who was exported to the USA and founded an important family there.

The Painswick Stud

During the same period Mrs E. M. Murray of Gloucestershire bought two mares from Lady Wentworth, Rishima (Radi ex Rishka) and Risslina, a daughter of Rafeef and Rissla, to join her stallion Sahban. Risslina proved to be a wonderful foundation mare, producing a succession of high-class fillies and colts by Crabbet and Hanstead stallions. Some of her daughters went to new breeders and founded other studs, while for many years her son Rifari was principal stallion at Painswick.

After Mrs Murray's death in 1957 her family continued to breed from the Painswick Arabians; her son and daughter-in-law, Mr and Mrs P. A. M. Murray, moved to Painswick Lodge with their own Foxbury Stud which they enlarged with descendants of Risslina.

The Agmerhurst Stud

Miss Mary Russell, who lived at Wisbech, was another indomitable enthusiast of the Arab horse, her admiration of the breed no doubt fostered by a father whose fine art collection included a perfect model of an Arabian, the work of a Russian refugee living in Bulgaria.

Lady Wentworth with Rissla (left) and her daughter Risslina (1926) by Rafeef, who became the foundation mare of Mrs E. M. Murray's Painswick Stud.

Roxan (1964) by Count Roland out of Bint Roxana (Greatheart ex Roxana) bred by Miss M. J. Stevens. Owned by Mr and Mrs J. R. Coward, Roxan was shown with success in ridden classes and became well known as the white horse in the White Horse Whisky Distillers advertisements: 'You can take a white horse anywhere' – as Roxan proved when photographed and filmed in many different places.

In 1931 she bought Ranya II (Redif ex Ranya) in foal to the Skowronek son, Ruskov. The resulting filly, Roxana, not only won high honours at the London Show but also bred a large number of foals which made an important contribution to English Arab horse breeding.

The Thriplow Stud

Another Cambridgeshire stud was founded in 1937 when Mrs Henry Walston of

Newton brought a stallion and three mares from her father J. M. Dickinson's well-known Traveler's Rest Stud in Tennessee.

The stallion, Jellaby, was of Egyptian breeding, his famous sire Nasr having been imported into the USA from the stud of Prince Ahmed Pasha Kemal and his dam being Prince Mohammed Ali's Hamama, a very well-known mare. Of the three mares Mrs Walston purchased, two were by Bazleyd, a son of Lal-I-Abdar, a famous sire bred in England by the Hon. George Savile and exported to the USA where his name was changed to Abu Zeyd.

The Thriplow Stud was disbanded in the 1960s but the horses were of particular interest since at that time Egyptian blood was rare in England. Their names now appear in the pedigrees of many Arabians including several good English racehorses.

The Biddesden Stud

One day in 1938 Lord and Lady Moyne paid a visit to Colonel Jenkins, and after lunch their host rode out his stallion, Raftan. According to their son, the Hon. Finn Guinness, the sight of the beautiful little grey was the inspiration behind his parents' decision to start breeding Arabians.

Soon afterwards they bought their first mare from Lady Wentworth, Starilla, by Rasim out of Star of the Hills. She was in foal to Naziri and duly produced a grey colt, Saladin II He had the distinction of being Naziri's only son to leave a male line; most of Naziri's foals were fillies and he died when comparatively young.

A second mare purchased from Lady Wentworth was Dafinetta, by Naziri out of the imported Dafina, and these two mares, together with Crystal Grey (Faris ex Silver Crystal) formed the foundation of the Biddesden Stud. It became a true family affair, with the sons riding Arab horses in the hunting field and in other performance spheres, including driving occasionally and polo at Cambridge.

The Well House Stud

Miss Margaret Greely grew up in India where she owned and rode Arabians and partbreds. One particularly lovely mare, Silvertail, she had rescued from starvation and ill treatment and some years later, after she had settled in England, she started breeding Arabians, having lost her heart to a three-year-old filly called Mihr-un-Nissa because of her resemblance to the beautiful Silvertail.

Not long before foaling Mihr-un-Nissa died and Miss Greely has always been grateful for the kindness shown her by Lady Yule who, hearing of her sad loss, invited her to Hanstead and offered her a mare from her stud. She chose Quaker Girl, by Riffal ex Niseyra, but disaster was to strike again when, not long after Quaker Girl's first foal was born, Miss Greely met with a serious accident at the Arab Horse Society Show at Roehampton, necessitating a year of complete rest and the break-up of her stud. Once again Lady Yule was there to help and when Miss Greely had fully recovered offered her a grey daughter of Grey Owl and Rikitea, whom she named Garance. Later two other mares from Hanstead, Teresita and Princess Zia, joined the Well House Stud and foals from these mares and their daughters have ensured the importance of the stud through their successes in England and abroad.

Author and life-long supporter of the true classic Arabian, Miss Greely is still breeding from a select number of mares at her home in Sussex.

The Barton Lodge Stud

The Barton Lodge Stud is distinguished by the fact that its importance is entirely due to the descendants of one mare – Nuhra, a Kehaileh Wadhnieh Khursanieh.

In 1938 HRH Princess Alice, a granddaughter of Queen Victoria, accompanied her husband the Earl of Athlone to Saudi Arabia in connection with the accession of King George VI. On their journey home they visited Bahrain, and the Sheikh, Hamed Al-Khalifa, presented them with a colt and a filly from the Royal Stud. The colt was later sold but Princess Alice presented the filly to her daughter, Lady May Abel-Smith. This filly, named Nuhra, became one of the great foundation mares of England.

During the war years Nuhra was bred to another import, Manak, then in the charge of the Secretary of the Arab Horse Society, Brigadier W. H. Anderson, at the Upend Stud in Newmarket. She produced two daughters by Manak, Nurmahal and Nurmana, and these fillies and their dam became the foundation mares of Sir Henry and Lady May Abel-Smith's stud when they returned to Barton Lodge, near Ascot, after the war was over in 1946.

Thereafter the Abel-Smiths sent their mares to Crabbet, Hanstead and Courthouse stallions to produce a succession of notable progeny. A number were exported to make their names abroad, but of those remaining in Britain mention should be made of Rabiha, dam of Ragos, a leading stallion in Scotland, and of

Sir Henry and Lady Abel-Smith's Darjeel (1962) by Dargee ex Rajella, at Kempton Park where he won the Male Championship for three successive years from 1968 to 1970 at the AHS Show, with George White

Rajella, whose sons Rajmek and Darjeel won a notable double at the AHS Show in 1965, when Rajmek won the male championship and Darjeel was champion colt. Later Darjeel achieved a post-war record by winning the male championship for three successive years, 1968–70, retiring from the show ring unbeaten. Rajmek and Darjeel both remained at Barton Lodge as principal stallions. Darjeel has sired many good horses including Dorial, the useful racehorse who is in turn the sire of winning racing Arabians.

However, the greatest of all the Barton Lodge mares was Zehraa, by Irex out of Nurmana. Not only was she the foundation of Mrs J. F. D. Trimingham's successful Grange Stud, but her daughter Razehra produced the good stallion Riaz, as well as

41

Alzehra, another top-class producer, and the outstanding mare Kazra, by Mikeno. Kazra, the foundation mare of Major and Mrs P. W. S. Maxwell's Lodge Farm Stud, founded a dynasty in her own right. Altogether four members of Zehraa's family have been winners of the coveted Princess Muna Saddle of Honour for family groups at the AHS Show.

The Blunt Stud

Lady Wentworth's daughter, Lady Anne Lytton, could remember as a child going round the horses at Crabbet with her grandmother Lady Anne Blunt, and she always had a passion for Arabians – as her brother said, Arab horses were in her blood. When Lady Wentworth acquired the Crabbet Stud she allowed both her daughters to choose two horses each and Lady Anne's first choice was the mare Ferda (from which she bred two foals) and the stallion Nasik, but her mother persuaded her to have instead the gelding Kaftan as she would get more enjoyment out of riding and driving him. Ferda and Nasik later went to the USA where they became two of the foremost Crabbet-bred horses in that country.

A few years later Lady Anne went abroad and then began her career at squash rackets; she also attended art school and became an accomplished artist. At this time there was a break in the relationship between Lady Anne and her mother. Many years later, in 1951, quite out of the blue Lady Wentworth presented Lady Anne with Mifaria, a mare by Oran out of Rithyana, as a birthday present. Four years afterwards Lady Anne inherited Newbuildings Place on the death of Miss Dorothy Carleton, who had been left a life tenancy there by Wilfrid Blunt. With Harry Cole and his wife Mary as her helpers Lady Anne moved into the old family home and started the Blunt Stud.

Mifaria proved an excellent brood mare, producing amongst others Manto by Blue Domino and El Meluk by Mikeno, and her daughter Mellawieh was the dam of the lovely Sahirah of the Storm. In due course Lady Anne saw and purchased the Polish-bred Grojec (Comet ex Gastronomia), who proved a good cross for her mares and a popular sire. But Lady Anne still hankered after a grey stallion of Crabbet blood-lines and when she saw the young colt Silver Flame (Indian Flame II ex Silver Ripple) at the Worth Stud she purchased a half-share in him. Progeny by these two stallions from Mifaria's descendants have been successful both in the show ring and as performance horses, and include a champion long-distance racehorse.

Lady Anne Lytton and her brother Anthony, 5th Earl of Lytton, with Peter Upton holding Silver Flame (1970, by Indian Flame II ex Silver Ripple) at the open day to celebrate the centenary of the Crabbet Stud, Newbuildings Place, Sussex, 9 June 1978.

All those who attended the Crabbet Centenary at Newbuildings in 1978 will have happy memories of a glorious summer day in the peaceful grounds. With its garden party atmosphere it was a delightful occasion for old friends to meet and enjoy wandering around the fine Carolean house, afterwards viewing the twenty Arabians of Crabbet descent which Lady Anne had invited to parade. The occasion will be remembered as a fitting climax to her life with Arab horses, for all too soon, after years of suffering from severe arthritis, which would have immobilised anyone of lesser determination, Lady Anne died following an operation.

Breeding in Britain since 1960

In this short resumé of more recent breeding it is not possible to mention more than a small number of outstanding Arabians and some of the more important studs in the period since 1960. The reason for taking this cut-off date is because in general it is since then that the greatest growth has been seen in the number of Arabians throughout the world – indeed, it could be called a population explosion.

That this rapid increase has been good for the breed is debatable. The dangers of indiscriminate breeding are considered in Chapter 8: however, on the positive side there are now many more high-quality animals to be found and Arabians are far more widely used as performance horses than in previous years.

One British stud of particular significance in this period is that belonging to Miss Patricia Lindsay. It was Miss Lindsay who first introduced Arabians from Poland after the war and began breeding from them at her Stockings Farm Stud. Her lovely imported mare Karramba (Witraz ex Karmen II) proved a highly successful foundation mare and with other stallions and mares imported from Poland added over the years her stud, now located in Devon, is of considerable importance to British breeders.

A stud in Norfolk founded with an imported Polish mare is that now owned by the Marquess Townshend. His wife, the late Marchioness Townshend, bought the very fine mare Nawarra (Trypolis ex Najada) in 1961 and put her to some of the best Crabbet stallions. Lady Townshend's Sky Arabians of Polish/English blood-lines are admired for their excellence as performance horses, as well as being successful in the show ring. Sky Crusader, by Grojec, was British National Champion Stallion in 1971 and in 1988 was the leading sire of Arab racehorses.

Another important Polish import selected by Miss Lindsay was the stallion Argos by Nabor (a grandson of Naseem) out of Arfa, who was a full sister to Bask. Argos came to England in 1961 and spent the last eight years of his life at Mr and Mrs Theobald's Yeld Bank Stud in Staffordshire. Argos was the only stallion since the war to have won in-hand and under saddle at the AHS Show in the same year. His influence as a sire can be seen in his many descendants which are found in a number of present-day studs, the largest collection being owned by Michael Harris in Devon.

One notable Argos son was Magic Argosy, bred by Mrs Roberts from her Indian Magic daughter, Fairy Magic. Another well-known stallion by Argos was Ragos, out of Rabiha of Barton Lodge breeding; he was owned by Mrs L. Macvie and was a prominent sire in Scotland.

Kazra, the truly great foundation mare of Major and Mrs P. W. S. Maxwell's Lodge Farm Stud in Oxfordshire, and already mentioned, was a daughter of Mikeno and was bred at Barton Lodge from Nuhra's great-granddaughter, Razehra. Over the years the Maxwells have used a number of imported stallions of Egyptian and Spanish blood-lines, the most notable being El Shaklan (Shaker el Masri ex Estopa), who was bred in Germany and is the sire, amongst others, of their leading stallion, Maleik el Kheil, whose dam Muneera is a granddaughter of Kazra.

Mikeno (Rissalix ex Namilla) was bred at Hanstead and purchased by Mr and Mrs H. Linney as a colt. He was the leading stallion at their Farnsfield Hall Stud and was a great show winner, well known for his brilliant action. Mikeno's numerous purebred, Anglo and partbred progeny have gone on to prove his value as a sire in performance as well as in the show ring.

An important stud which was founded with Hanstead-bred horses is that belonging to Major and Mrs T. W. I. Hedley at Windermere. They bought, amongst others, General Grant and Count Rapello and the mares Umatella and Samaveda when Miss Wolf was selling the Hanstead Arabians. Their Briery Close Stud has produced numerous show winners, whose descendants have proved important in many other studs. General Lee Gold, a grandson of General Grant, owned by Mrs Fox-Kibby, was one of the first purebred Arabians to be placed in affiliated three-day events.

Mr and Mrs D. D. Wright purchased the previously mentioned Ludo (Blue Domino ex Rithyana) as a yearling and with the Indian Magic daughter, Indian Starlight, as their foundation mare built up an important collection of Crabbet blood-lines at their Moulton Arabian Stud in Norfolk.

Also in Norfolk the late Mrs Alison Hardcastle bred the Indian Magic son, Scindian Magic, from her mare Scindia by Rithan ex Senga. He stood at her Mill Farm Arabian Stud and in addition to purebreds sired a large number of outstanding Anglo-Arabs and partbreds. Scindian Magic's progeny and descen-

Opposite page (*top*)
Mrs K. Fox-Kibby's General Lee Gold (1980) by General Gold out of Leda, bred by Miss M. Roberts. He has competed successfully at Senior affiliated level in horse trials, show jumping and dressage. In 1991 he was selected to stand at the Muschamp Stallion Station for carefully selected, top-quality competition stallions, the first Arabian to join this exclusive group of horses.

Opposite page (*bottom*)
Mr and Mrs D. D. Wright's foundation sire Ludo (1953) by Blue Domino ex Rithyana, bred by B. Dixon. An important sire, Ludo also had considerable success in the show ring and was Supreme Ridden Champion Riding Horse at the Royal International at the White City in 1963.

dants have been instrumental in promoting Arabian blood in performance horses; one of his grandsons is the Olympic dressage horse, Prince Consort.

Two studs which rose to fame after Lady Wentworth's death but which no longer exist are those which belonged to the late Mrs E. M. Thomas and Mr M. A. Pitt-Rivers. Mrs Thomas kept only mares at Metcombe, in Devon, and she started her stud with two Dargee daughters acquired from Lady Wentworth, Rissalma and Incoronetta. Later she bought others from Cecil Covey including Silver Sheen and Silent Wings, whose son Azraq by Blue Domino was sold to Africa as a young horse. Azraq was a loss to British breeding since his only son and daughter in England, Silver Blue and Blue Sylphide, have bred very high-class progeny notable for passing on his superb action. Blue Sylphide was owned by Mrs N. Brogden and her daughter Mrs C. Stamper, whose Beacon Arabian Stud in Cumbria produces fine stock.

The Tollard Park Stud, owned by Michael Pitt-Rivers, was also founded with horses purchased mainly from Crabbet, or of Crabbet blood-lines. His principal foundation mare, Indian Snowflake (Ludo ex Indian Starlight), was bred by the Wrights; she was the dam of Haroun by Hanif and Nimet by Iridos, both big show winners. Other notable horses bred at Tollard Royal include Nasib and Sabek. Mr Pitt-Rivers had to disband his stud due to ill health in 1986 but a few years earlier he had imported from Australia Ralvon Elijah, who sprang to fame when winning the British National Championship in 1984 and 1985. Elijah was subsequently sold to a syndicate and exported to the USA.

Hanif, by Silver Vanity out of Sirella, bred by Mr Covey and now owned by Mr G. Plaister, has appeared regularly in the Veteran Class at the AHS Show. He has become a great favourite with audiences and his win in 1991 at the age of 29 was greeted with tremendous applause.

The Duchess of Rutland also started breeding with mares purchased from Mr Covey when he disbanded the Crabbet Stud; the well-known stallion Bright Shadow (Radi ex Pale Shadow) ended his days in the Rutland Stud. One of his granddaughters, the lovely Silver Circlet, has on five occasions won her class at the annual summer show. The principal stallions at present at Rutland are Bright Crown (Bright Shadow ex Crowning Glory) and Silvern Idyll, whose sire Masjid (Bright Shadow ex Naxindra) was owned by Mrs B. K. Moss in his later life.

Mr and Mrs R. M. Kydd had the Oran son, Indian King, at their Cruglas Stud in Wales during the 1960s and 1970s and bred some good horses by him out of the Dargee twins Dancing Sunlight and Dancing Shadow. One of the most important mares of this breeding was the lovely Tarantella, foundation mare of Diana Whittome's stud, also in Wales. Further south Mr and Mrs J. R. Coward have bred some good stock by their stallion Roxan, who is a descendant of Miss Mary Russell's mare Roxana.

Mr and Mrs P. A. M. Murray have continued their Foxbury Stud at Painswick and imported the stallion Bremervale Emperor from Australia some years ago to breed to their mares of mainly Risslina descent. Mr Murray's sister, Mrs J. Bowring, had for some years the two great show mares Silver Grey and Silver Sheen and bred some notable horses from them.

The previously mentioned Harwood Stud, owned by Mrs Monica Calvert, is now approaching its centenary and hopefully will continue for many more years as a family concern since her daughter and son-in-law, Mr and Mrs J. Moore, and their children are all keenly interested. Harwood Stud usually has one or two Arabians racing, trained by Mrs Moore.

Dotted around Britain are numerous smaller studs, many of which have bred Arabians of significance. It is not possible here to give more than a few, but amongst the many mares and stallions Mr and Mrs F. Smith's beautiful mare, Star of Destiny, by the Polish stallion Grojec out of Royal Destiny, stands out; she has won a number of major championships. The Worth Stud had the Silver Vanity daughter Silver Ripple, dam of Silvern Dream and of British National Champion Silver Flame, who spent his last years with Mr and Mrs D. Bretherton at their Hawkhurst Stud. Silver Flame's lovely daughter Azeme Bint Gleam, bred and owned by Mrs J. Kirch, has produced several top-class sons and daughters including the outstanding sire Aboud, recently exported to Abu Dhabi.

Silver Vanity (1950) by Oran out of Silver Gilt, the famous daughter of Indian Gold and Silver Fire. One of the finest stallions ever bred by Lady Wentworth, he was twice British National Champion. After Lady Wentworth's death he was exported to the USA but he left important descendants in England.

Mrs J. H. Paine had on lease the American-bred Ben Rabba, of Nasik descent through his sire, from which promising lines are developing through two of his sons, while his granddaughter, Aureme, a half sister to Aboud, was the in-hand champion at the 1990 AHS Show.

Mrs Trimingham for some years had the successful Grange Stud in Lincolnshire where she stood Melchior, bred in Germany of Egyptian blood-lines. The Silverdale Stud belonging to Mr and Mrs R. R. Carr has produced a large number of show winners with horses of Egyptian, Polish and English blood-lines. Mrs J. Ratcliff has successfully bred purebreds and Anglo-Arabs for many years; she is a leading breeder in Arab racing and has been using Russian stallions with success in this field. Another breeder crossing Russian and English-bred Arabians with the idea of letting them prove their worth on the racecourse is Mrs J. Kadri, whose stud is comparatively new; she has a good young sire of Russian breeding, Narim, by Moment ex Nejnaia.

49

4 Arab breeding around the world

Since 1960 the interchange of stock amongst Arab horse breeders has increased so much that many Arabians carry in their pedigrees blood-lines from several countries. Of course the breed originated in the deserts of Arabia but it is becoming exceedingly rare to find a stud concentrating on the descendants of one particular group of original imported Arabians, or even on those from one of the early great studs. The terms 'Russian', 'Spanish', 'Egyptian', 'Polish', can, therefore, be misleading and should be used only to describe the country in which the animal was bred, or in which its immediate ancestors live.

The recent political upheavals in Eastern Europe and the USSR, too, sow further confusion as regions declare themselves independent nation states. For our purposes, therefore, political distinctions (e.g. Russia and the USSR) have been made in this chapter but breeding distinctions have been retained as historically used (e.g. Russian-bred not Soviet-bred).

Germany

One of the oldest Arab studs still in existence is the State Stud of Marbach, in Germany. It began when King William I of Württemberg came to the throne in 1816 and decided to start a stud at Weil. A national stud already existed at Marbach where Arab stallions had been used for many years, but King William intended to breed purebred Arabians and he set about acquiring mares as well as stallions for his Royal Stud at Weil.

He is said to have had two aims, to breed purebred Arabians for saddle horses of quality and powerful performance, and to breed halfbreds with a strong Oriental content, for taller and equally powerful carriage horses. Persian and Caucasian horses were used intially for cross-breeding, but it was later found that the best results were achieved by putting Thoroughbred mares to Arab stallions.

Some of the Arabian foundation stock came direct from Arabia, while others were bought from various studs in Europe. The most famous acquisition was the stallion Bairactar, who was imported from Arabia by Baron von Fechtig and purchased by King William. He was to prove an extremely important foundation sire and a large number of his sons and daughters remained at Weil. One of his descendants, Amurath 'Weil' 1881, with many crosses to Bairactar in his pedigree, had a colossal influence on Arab horse breeding in Europe. At the age of 14 Amurath went to the Austrian Stud where he sired a prodigious number of foals and is said to have remained fertile up to his death at the age of 30.

Another purchase from Baron Fechtig was Murana I, whose line is the oldest in Europe, with descendants still alive today. The king's equerry, Von Hugel,

The desert-bred grey Bairactar, imported by Baron von Fechtig in 1816 and bought by the King of Württemberg. The most important foundation sire at Weil, through his many sons and daughters Bairactar was probably Europe's most influential stallion.

Mansul, by Sawih Ibn Wisznu ex Mekka, of Marbach/Achental breeding, owned by the Saalegrund Stud of Germany. Reserve Champion at Aachen, 1982 and 1985, German National Champion 1987.

acquired the grey mares Saklavia and Koheil Aguse from the Abbas Pasha collection. The latter was to be of great importance for the Babolna Stud through her son, Amurath-Bairactar.

When King William I died in 1864 there were over 70 horses in the Royal Stud, which was continued by his successor Carl, who reigned until 1891. The demand at that time was for horses for agricultural work and the stud began to deteriorate, although Amurath was foaled during Carl's reign. Carl was succeeded by William II who was more interested in Thoroughbreds and the number of Arabians began to dwindle. On his death the Royal Stud passed to his daughter Princess Pauline, and she tried to find fresh blood to rejuvenate the stud. Eventually the stallion Jasir was bought for her by the German Carl Raswan, an Arab horse devotee who settled in the USA, from Prince Mohammed Ali of Egypt, but the great depression of the early 1930s forced her to make over the stud to the State of Württemberg.

Most of the horses moved to Marbach and over the years the State Stud was built up again so that by 1990 there were over 60 purebred Arabians. Amongst more recent acquisitions mention must be made of Hadban Enzahi, who with his half-sister, Nadja, arrived at Marbach in 1955 from El Zahraa in Egypt. Hadban Enzahi was by the famous Nazeer and he has had a great influence on the stud. In 1990 a Polish stallion, Penthagon by Gwarny, was leased, thus restoring the Bairactar sire line which had been lost for over 100 years.

There are now a number of private studs in Germany, one of the most important being Om el Arab, for it is there that El Shaklan was bred. El Shaklan, by Shaker El Masri out of Estopa, and thus of Egyptian and Spanish blood-lines, was leased to England for two seasons as a young horse before being exported to the USA. His stock have had resounding successes in the show ring in Europe and he is said to have almost revolutionised German breeding.

Herr Ismer, who owns one of the oldest private studs, was amongst the first to import Polish horses into Germany and currently has one of the largest establishments. Dr Nagel greatly influenced the breeding of Egyptian lines and brought in Ansata Halim Shah. Herr Koch, however, has developed what is known as the 'German Cross' at his Saalegrund Stud. This is largely achieved by breeding solely from the original foundation lines of the country; a case, one might say, of going full circle – a situation which shows signs of developing in other studs around the world.

Hungary

In addition to ranking as another of the oldest studs in Europe, the State Stud of Babolna in Hungary must be the one which has suffered more upheavals than any other, yet has survived.

In 1789 the Hungarian Treasury purchased a 30,000 acre estate on the principal highway to Vienna, in an area of rolling plains, and built a stud, though it was not until 1806 that any number of horses were kept there. From that date stud books were maintained, recording the history of the horses; and the stud is still considered the centre of horse-breeding in Hungary.

Soon after Babolna's inception war necessitated the evacuation of the horses to Mezöhegyes, and Napoleon's invading French army, furious at the loss of valuable equine booty, set fire to the buildings. By 1816 Babolna was once again functioning as a stud but with the main purpose of producing partbred Arabians, mostly by using purebred stallions (many of which were looted from a French stallion station) on Hungarian field-bred mares. However, amongst the imported Arabians one mare, Adjuze, has left a family still extant. In 1833 an epidemic decimated the stock but it was decided to persevere with the breeding of Arabians and importations were made from Syria which included the important purebred stallion Shagya, from whom the separate breed of Shagyas are descended (see p. 110 below).

By 1845 there were about 500 horses of all kinds in the stud when another epidemic, followed by revolution and war, imposed a further period of upheaval and disruption to breeding.

Then in 1852 the Emperor Franz Joseph became interested in Babolna and he appointed Colonel Von Brudermann to command an expedition to the Middle East to obtain more Arabians. Von Brudermann was said to have an excellent eye for a horse and in a journey which lasted nearly two years he succeeded in bringing into Hungary 16 stallions and 50 mares, 14 of which were in foal, and of these 14 stallions and 32 mares were assigned to Babolna. Brudermann advocated breeding just purebreds, but he was commandant at Babolna only until 1860 and his successors disregarded his advice and reverted to partbreds again – known as 'Arab Race' in Hungary.

In 1869 the Emperor assigned Babolna to the Hungarian Government and a commission was appointed to decide policy. The period up to the First World War was an important one for the stud and saw the acquisition, amongst others, of Gazlan. He was foaled in 1864 at Lipica of desert-bred parents, and was to found the great Gazal line.

During much of this time Babolna was under the management of Fadlallah el Hedad, until his death in 1924; he was an Arab who came to Europe in 1857 with the Brudermann importations. It is said that the 14-year-old, then named Nagle, was loath to be parted from his father's horse when it was sold and so joined Brudermann's party. An attractive intelligent lad, he was spotted by the Emperor and was admitted to the military college from which he passed out as an officer. He changed his name, worked his way up in the Austro-Hungarian Army and, via the remount service, eventually became commandant at Babolna. It was Fadlallah el

Champion Shagya mare bred at Babolna, Ghalion-II (1973) by the purebred Ghalion out of 44 Shagya XXXVI.

Hedad who was responsible for importing in 1885 the black O'Bajan, who was one of Hungary's most valuable stallions, and Koheilan, whose line has been influential in many other European countries; and in 1902 Siglavy-Bagdady, another very important stallion.

In the Romanian invasion of 1919 Babolna again suffered. Some of the horses were evacuated but the Romanians stole all they could. After the war the task of building up the stud began once more, and Babolna entered another pre-eminent era under General Tibor von Pettko-Szandtner, who was commandant from 1932 to 1942. A great stallion of this period was Kuhailan Zaid, purchased by Bogdan von Zientarski, the Polish Prince Roman Sanguszko's manager, from the Middle

East and said to be one of the best stallions ever brought from the desert. A reservoir of purebreds was maintained from which the Lipizzana and partbred Arab was reinforced and Babolna was reputed as the 'Mecca of European Arab breeding'.

In the Second World War Babolna suffered yet again. As the Red Army advanced the horses were scattered: some to Germany, some to Poland; many were auctioned. In 1947 the remnants were re-united at Babolna but difficulties in repairing damaged buildings and finding staff, together with confused policies, hampered progress. It was not until 1960 that Babolna once more became a well-organised, successful establishment. A fresh impetus was given to the stud with imports from Egypt, notable amongst them being the stallions Ibn Galal and Farag.

Babolna has recently had a change of management and, being the original home of the Shagyas, a decision has been taken to concentrate on that breed and reduce the number of purebred Arabians.

Poland

The pedigrees of Polish Arabians date from 1803, the year in which Prince Jerome Sanguszko organised an expedition to Arabia to buy horses. He was followed by Count Waclaw Rzewuski who, after pursuing Oriental studies, travelled to Arabia and lived for some time with the Bedouin, absorbing many of their ideals. He collected 130 Arab horses which, after an adventurous journey, he brought back to Eastern Europe for his stud at Sawran, and for other studs in Poland, Russia and Germany.

The Sanguszko family continued to own large numbers of horses, including many of Oriental blood, and it was Prince Hieronymus Sanguszko who reorganised the large family estate south-east of Kiev and founded the Slawuta Stud. In 1818 his son, Eustachy-Erazm, succeeded in importing a batch of Arabians, including the stallion Hajlan, acquired for him in Arabia by his equerry.

When Count Eustachy-Erazm died in 1845 the stud was divided between his son Roman the Elder and the latter's daughter Maria, who was married to Count Alfred Potocki and to whom he left Antoniny, a large estate nearly 100 miles south of Slawuta. These two studs, maintained by the same family for three generations, had a great influence on Polish Arab horse breeding of that period.

Over the years a steady stream of desert-bred Arabians were added to both studs. Prince Roman bought near Aleppo the famous stallion Batran-Agha; Abu

Hejl and Ezrak-Seglawi also went to Slawuta and left very fine descendants. The studs became famous throughout Europe and visitors came to see and buy.

The Blunts visited the Potockis in 1884 and were greatly impressed with the horses, a large number of which were grey. Wilfrid Blunt stayed again the next year and on another trip in 1895 he also saw the Sanguszko Stud, which he described as really splendid, remarking particularly on the number of flea-bitten grey mares, with 'more flea-bites than grey' – a feature of many of today's Polish mares.

Eighteen years later the American-born sculptor and pistol shot Walter Winans went on a shooting visit to Antoniny. He was enchanted with the horses and wanted to buy a team of four driving Arabians. He was dissuaded and instead purchased a young grey stallion by the imported Ibrahim which caught his eye in the stables – and thus the famous Skowronek came to England.

The Slawuta and Antoniny Studs both perished in the political upheavals of 1917; many horses were destroyed and the elderly Prince Roman was murdered. Another famous early stud was that of the Counts Branicki, but this also perished in the same period. A third family who contributed to early Polish breeding were the Counts Dzieduszycki who owned the famous grey stallion Bagdad. In 1843 Count Juliusz Dzieduszycki went to the Middle East and spent two years there, returning to Jarczowce with Abu Hejl, half brother to Batran-Agha, and the mares Gazella (who went to Slawuta), Mlecha and Sahara, the three great Polish foundation mares from which a high proportion of present-day Arabians descend in the female line.

After the First World War the emphasis on purebred Arab breeding switched to the State Studs. Stock of the old privately owned studs began to be collected at Janow-Podlaski, east of Warsaw, in 1919. The Polish Arab Association, founded in 1926, had as its secretary Dr Edward Skorkowski, whose contribution to Arab horse breeding in Poland has been immense. His first task was to collate information for the Polish Stud Book and to organise races for Arabians. The idea behind racing was not to find the fastest horses but to test constitution, soundness and temperament. It was felt important to ensure there was no degeneration in characteristics of endurance and performance ability, so breeding stock was selected with these in mind, as well as for conformation and type.

The other main State Studs were at Nowy Dwor, south of Crakow, Albigowa on the former Potocki estate in the south-east of the country, and Michalow, south-west of Warsaw. Building on the foundation stock of the pre-war private studs plus additions brought in from Babolna and Weil, Arab horse breeding in Poland

57

Winner of the Polish Derby in 1933, the stallion Kaszmir, by Farys II ex Hedba, bred in 1929 at the Janow State Stud.

flourished between the wars with stallions such as Baksysz, Abu Mlech, Enwer Bey, Fetysz, Koheilan I and Ofir prominent, together with the mares Gazella II, Koalicja, Siglavi-Bagdady, Hebda and Pomponia.

The Second World War caused yet more havoc, with horses evacuated, studs overrun by advancing armies and buildings destroyed. After the war the Poles again set about restoring their studs. With unquenchable devotion and persistence

Arabian mares at the Michalow Stud in Poland.

they built them up once more to an excellence which attracted buyers from the USA and all parts of Europe, so that by the 1970s Polish Arabians were very much in demand. Some of the principal horses to emerge since the war are Doktryner, Czort, Wielki Szlem, Trypolis, Nabor (imported from the USSR and later sold to the USA) and mares such as Bandola and Carmen.

Arab horse breeding in Poland today is still in the hands of the Government but

Etogram (1981) by El Paso ex Etruria by Palas, an example of 'modern' Polish breeding (combining old Polish lines with outcrosses to such horses as the Egyptian-bred Aswan who was a very important sire in Russia). Etogram was chief sire at the Kurozwélei State Stud.

traditions established by the early private breeders are continued in the State Studs. However, as in any Civil Service administration, there are inevitably conflicts of interest when commercial aspects have to be considered in policy-making.

As American breeders began buying Polish-breds and demand for them grew rapidly in the 1970s, so prices escalated and exportation became a valuable source of foreign currency for Poland. Annual Prestige Sales were held at Janow-Podlaski and attracted a number of foreign buyers; in the early days they were mostly from the USA. This led to quite a few stallions going abroad and as a result some valuable sire-lines have been lost through the sale of the progenitor before suitable sons have become established for continuance.

However, Poland has a wealth of superb mares, many of which have taken top honours in European show rings. Grey appears to be the predominant colour and such mares as Pilarka (Palas ex Pierzga), Pikita (Probat ex Platyna), Europa (Bandos ex Eunice) and Egina (Palas ex Estrada) are only a few which have been prominent in recent years; Piewica, imported from the USSR, is the founder of the currently most successful mare line. An earlier mare who had had a great influence is Elza, the dam of three important sisters, Celina, Ellora and Elzunia. Principal stallions to have emerged since the war include Witraz, Comet, Bandos and Palas.

Although many Arabians in the USSR and Poland share the same ancestors it would appear that in general each country is seeking to produce a slightly different type. The Polish Arabians show a certain elegance particularly noticeable in the head; whilst the Russian-bred horses are often larger and more powerfully built.

Russia

Both Russians and Poles had comparatively easy access to Arabia and, as was the case with Polish Arab studs, the earliest breeders in Russia imported large numbers of Arabians. However, serious breeding of purebreds did not begin in Russia until the end of the nineteenth century.

In 1888 Prince Sherbatov and his wife, Princess Olga Alexandrovna, set off with her brother, Count Stroganov, for Syria and the North Arabian desert, where they proposed to study the Arab horse in its natural habitat. They travelled amongst some of the best-known horse-breeding tribes and purchased a number of mares and stallions from them as foundation stock for the Stroganov stud near Tersk, in the northern Caucasus. On a second journey Count Stroganov bought three more mares in or around Damascus.

The stated policy of the stud was 'to breed Arabians of unquestionable blood' and to improve the native Kabarda by cross-breeding with Arabians. The owners of the stud believed that it was important to preserve the typical characteristics of the Arabian and that this could only be done if the youngstock were reared in a climate similar to that of their native land, which the Northern Caucasian foothills of the

Kabarda region provided. They noted that with more careful upbringing and the addition of oats to diet the youngsters tended to grow two or three inches taller than the original desert-bred foundation stock. They also observed that if young Arabians were not given sufficient exercise their growth was retarded.

During the Russian Revolution and Civil War most of the private studs were liquidated, but in 1921 the Soviet state set up a stud at Tersk, on the old Stroganov and Sultan-Girea estates. At first the breeding was indiscriminate but with the arrival in 1930 of the Babolna stallion Koheilan IV and of Kann and six mares from France the Soviet authorities were encouraged to develop the purebred section, and in 1936 a delegation from the Department of Horsebreeding went to the Crabbet Stud.

On the first visit Lady Wentworth was not aware that the Soviets were possible buyers; they had merely asked to see the horses and so were shown many of the best. Impressed with the parade, the visitors returned and it emerged that they were keen to purchase in large numbers. Then the bargaining began!

Following the 1930s slump the Crabbet Stud, like many others, was in need of funds; a big sale abroad could solve Lady Wentworth's financial problems, but she was not prepared to sell her best horses. The negotiations continued over several days, with Lady Wentworth established in one room and the Soviets in another, while Geoffrey Covey, her stud manager, acted as a go-between. The horses selected for negotiation were examined with extreme care by the Soviets, who even secreted themselves in the stables with the horses for private investigations behind closed doors! Finally agreement was reached and six stallions and nineteen mares went to Tersk. Lady Wentworth was sorry to lose Naseem, although she did have his full brother Naziri, but it was the sale of so many of her mares that really grieved her. Although she refused to part with her best those that went were a loss to the Crabbet Stud.

This sale made a most important contribution to Arab horse breeding in the USSR and when, in 1939, the pick of the Polish stock at Janow-Podlaski, including Ofir, Piolun, Enwer Bey and the mares Gazella II, Plotka and Elegantka, fell into Soviet hands, Tersk became firmly established.

After the war the stud flourished. Once political prejudice was overcome and the Russian Arab Stud Book entrants were accepted by the USA, there began a great demand in the USA for the Tersk horses. More recently Russian-bred horses have come to Europe in ever increasing numbers.

Stallions which have had a large influence on modern breeding are Aswan, Arax and his son, Nabeg. Aswan (Nazeer ex Yosreia) was bred in Egypt in 1958 and given to the USSR by President Nasser as a token of appreciation for the technical assistance given to Egypt by the USSR during the construction of the Aswan dam on the Nile. Others of importance include Moment, Menes and Naslednik. Amongst the mares Neposeda (Priboj ex Nonemklature), foaled in 1955, and

Palas (1968) by Aswan ex Panel by Nil, of 'new' Russian breeding. Palas was purchased by Poland and became chief sire at Janow-Podlaski. One of the most important stallions in Poland, Palas was known as 'the Sire of Champions'.

Monopolia (Priboj ex Mammona), foaled a year later, have become especially influential in modern Tersk pedigrees.

For over 30 years Russian-bred Arabians have been raced as youngsters to test them for soundness and speed; any horse that breaks down is usually excluded from the breeding stock. The horses begin racing as two-year-olds and are classified into groups, with the races taking place on a dirt track at one racecourse, the weekly meetings being shared with Thoroughbreds.

Spain

It was not until the beginning of the twentieth century that any real effort was made to breed purebred Arabians in Spain. A State Stud had been established by royal order on a leased estate in Cordoba in 1893. The Yeguada Militar, or Army Stud, was founded for the breeding of Andalusians but the policy was to upgrade them with Arabian stallions. A few years later it was decided to enlarge the Arabian section, and with stallions and mares purchased from Poland and Egypt as well as Syria the breeding of purebreds began in earnest.

A few private studs also existed, the most important being that of the Duke of Veragua. He imported horses from Argentina, France and Poland and then purchased three stallions and thirteen mares from England, including five daughters of Skowronek. The Duke's horses quickly made a name for themselves and some stallions acquired by the state were bred on the Veragua Stud.

During the Spanish Civil War the Duke of Veragua was murdered and the stud papers burnt. The Yeguada Militar collected together a number of his mares, all of which were branded, but without detailed information it was not possible accurately to ascertain the identity of most of the horses. Therefore the mares were given new names starting with the prefix 'Ver', and they made an important contribution to Arab horse breeding in Spain.

In the mid 1950s the Yeguada Militar was moved to a former remount depot near Jerez de la Frontera and at that time some of the Arabians were sold. Several private studs were started up and pure breeding in Spain flourished with the lines of Barquillo, Maquillo and Congo featuring amongst the most important.

Private studs have continued to increase in number and there is now less need to depend on the Yeguada Militar for stallions and foundation stock. New breeders have brought in or leased horses of mainly Egyptian lines, although the British-bred Carmargue (White Lightning ex Velvet Shadow) was leased to Spain for three seasons; he subsequently went on lease to the USA for a further three years. Generally speaking Spanish breeders have kept their studs freer from an influx of imported horses than many other countries.

Rest of Europe

Nearly every country in Europe favouring the Arab horse has experienced the same dramatic increase in numbers as in Britain and the USA.

In Sweden, for example, there were in the early 1960s about 20 Arabians: twenty years later the number had risen to some 3,000. The Netherlands has a rather older history of Arab horse breeding, with nearly all its early foundation stock coming from England. Recently in a few of the large Dutch studs interest has switched to Russian-bred horses, and at some to Polish blood-lines. France, more particularly famous for her Anglo-Arabs, has an increasing number of private breeders with purebred studs. Belgium, strongly influenced by the Netherlands, has begun to make a significant contribution to European purebred breeding. Italy has a small but enthusiastic group of breeders, who have built up a stock of breeding animals by importation since the late 1970s.

Australia

Horses were not indigenous to Australia and were first introduced by Europeans late in the eighteenth century. The earliest imports came from the Cape of Good Hope and by 1800 the Government of New South Wales had 30 horses at the Crown Stud at Toongabbie. They were of a somewhat nondescript type, described as mainly fit for light harness work and riding.

The Governor of the Colony, Philip Gidley King, became concerned at the number of inferior horses in the country and began making enquiries for a high-class Arabian to upgrade stock. He was told that he would not get anything good enough for less than £200 sterling (a considerable sum then) in India, where at the time there were many dealers importing horses from the Arabian peninsula, and he reluctantly decided that money would have to be spent if he was to procure a good enough stallion.

In 1804 the stallion Shark arrived in Sydney and became the first known Arabian to stand at the Crown Stud. His name figures prominently in the pedigree of many early racehorses and his daughters were increasingly bred back to him. Shark was followed by another Arabian, White William, who was sent to Van Diemen's Land, as Tasmania was then called.

Some of the pedigrees of horses bred from these Arabians were kept and later incorporated in the Australian Stud Book, but when it was decided to exclude from this horses other than recognised racing families no central registry for Arabians was formed and these blood-lines were lost for purebred breeding. However, the Arabians imported before 1830 improved the stock so noticeably that Australian horse breeders gained a high reputation overseas. The 'Waler' from New South Wales became popular in India for Army remounts and also for racing.

Following the gold rush in the 1850s horses were turned loose to run wild and fend for themselves, with the inevitable result of deterioration in quality. Although a few breeders maintained their studs the majority of people needing horses found it easier and cheaper to round up a few hundred 'brumbies' and break them in.

In order to revitalise the light horse breeds in Australia more Arabian stallions and a few mares were imported. As 'full blood' horses (as Arabians and Thoroughbreds were described) they would have been eligible for a special section in the Australian Stud Book for Thoroughbred racehorses – as was then the case in the General Stud Book of England – but already there was a prejudice against Arabians, English Thoroughbreds being preferred as superior racehorses.

In the 1870s several breeders were using Arabian sires and encouraging breeders to put their larger Thoroughbred mares to them. Amongst them were Messrs W. J. and A. A. Dangar who in 1874 commissioned Captain Roger Upton to go to Arabia and procure a stallion for their stud. He purchased a three-year-old colt, Alif, for the Dangars which was sent via England to Australia to arrive in time for the 1875 season.

The oldest family of purebred Arabians registered in Australia today is, however, descended from one of the Sir James Penn Boucaut imports of 1891. Elected to the House of Assembly in 1861, Boucaut was made Premier of South Australia in 1867 and in 1878 he was appointed judge of the Supreme Court. One of his main recreations was his Arab stud, kept on his estate at the foot of Mount Barker in South Australia.

In June 1888 Sir James spotted an Australian newspaper notice advertising a forthcoming Auction Sale of 8 stallions and 12 mares by Wilfrid Blunt at Crabbet Park. He was to buy Rafyk (Azrek ex Rose of Sharon) and two daughters of Kars, Rose of Jericho out of Rodania, and Dahna ex Dahma. Rose of Jericho produced a string of colts which went as station sires, but a female line was established from

Dahna. Reinforced later by the importation of her daughter El Zahr, by Miss Dillon's Imamzada, the Dahna family became important 'down under'. Sir James also imported Faroun and the mare Namusa, and she too established a significant and extensive family.

Horses from Boucaut's Quambi Stud were sold to all parts of Australia, but when Sir James eventually decided to give up horse breeding due to ill health a large number of his Arabians were bought by the Hon. Samuel Winter-Cooke of Victoria. However, after the dispersal sale of Winter-Cooke's horses in 1928 many of the best became lost to purebred breeding, as the Arab Horse Society of Australia had yet to be formed, though a few breeders were registering their animals in England.

In 1925 Mr A. E. Grace imported from England the well-known endurance horse Shahzada, together with Nejdmich, a desert-bred mare, and Miriam, of Crabbet blood-lines. Shahzada was for eight successive years champion Arab stallion at the Sydney Royal Easter Show. Another early breeder was Jos. F. Jelbart; when the New South Wales Department of Agriculture purchased 18 mares from him in 1949 all of them traced to Shahzada, whose influence through sons and daughters of Nejdmieh and Miriam spread throughout the country.

One of the most important and still existing studs in Australia is Fenwick, Victoria. It was established by Mrs A. D. D. Maclean in 1925 and in addition to acquiring descendants of early imports, thus saving them for posterity, she brought in many horses from England. She also purchased other British-bred Arabians in Australia, making her stud one of the largest in the country.

Notable amongst the first horses acquired by Dora Maclean were the stallion Indian Light and mares Rafina, Nuralina and Nasirich. In 1947 Mrs Maclean came over to England and visited Hanstead as well as Crabbet. At Hanstead she made one of her most significant purchases, the tall bay stallion Riffal, whose contribution to Australian Arab horse breeding was immense. Others of importance included the Crabbet-bred stallions Shafreyn and Silver Moonlight, and the mares Rosinella and Royal Radiance; whilst one of her last importations, the chestnut Sindh from Crabbet, is another stallion to have left his mark.

Many studs, too numerous to list here, were founded with Fenwick stock, though mention should be made of the Ennerdale Stud started by Mrs Jean Luckock, and Mrs Elwyn Bligh's Bostock Stud, whose British import from Miss Margaret Greely, Scherazade, went out in foal to Blue Domino.

Another early stud was that of Mrs Mary Leicht, who began by breeding from

The Australian-bred Ralvon Elijah (1978) by Ralvon Nazarene ex Mill Hill Sharmal, bred by Ron and Val Males and imported as a colt by M. A. Pitt-Rivers. He was sold to the USA when the Tollard Royal Stud was disbanded. Elijah was British National Champion in 1984 and 1985. (Note his well-trained stance, alert and with happy expression.)

Opposite page (*top*)
Sirdar, at four years old in Australia, a son of Chahando and the desert-bred mare, Neldnich.

Opposite page (*bottom*)
Barada II, by Raisuli out of Gadara, with Baksheesh, filly by Rakib. Barada founded one of the largest and most important families in Australia. She was bred by A. J. McDonald and was bought in 1945 by Mrs A. D. D. Maclean.

Jelbart mares but later imported Silver Magic and the two stallions Silwan and Spindrift from Crabbet. When she retired from breeding Mrs Leicht's horses were all acquired by the Queensland (Gatton) College, to whom she had offered them. The New South Wales Department of Agriculture studs at Hawkesbury and Wagga Wagga imported Sala from Hanstead and Razaz from Courthouse in England, and several new breeders purchased their foundation stock from these studs.

The 1970s and 1980s have been described as decades of breeding experiment in Australia, which is largely made up of a great many small studs. Generally speaking the old mare lines predominate, with 'newer' blood brought in through stallions. One exception has been the Russian-bred mare Naadirah, who successfully unites Egyptian and European blood-lines. She has given both Australia and New Zealand valuable male and female breeding stock.

The stallions which have made their mark in recent years are of differing blood-lines; they include Mustapha (Hadban Enzahi ex Masarrah) of Egyptian lines but bred in Germany, Sindh (Silver Vanity ex Silfina) and Greylight (Bright Shadow ex Royal Radiance), both from Crabbet, Royal Domino (Blue Domino ex Scherazade) imported *in utero*, Ambition (Bask ex Bint Ambara) of Polish breeding, and the home-bred Ralvon Pilgrim (Rikham ex Trix Silver). In addition, a stallion which has made an impact through several excellent imported sons and a daughter is the German-bred El Shaklan.

Arabians and their derivatives have been promoting the breed in a variety of performance events in the last few years. In 1987 a partbred gelding named Tutankhamon won the Haig Cup, Australia's highest dressage award, and Arabians dominate endurance riding, which is a flourishing sport in the country. They are being used increasingly in eventing, also in harness, especially in cross country and team events, and it is looked upon as a healthy sign for the breed that the level of competition amongst ridden Arabians has steadily risen.

New Zealand

New Zealand is one of the most recent countries to start breeding Arabians seriously, but there is no doubt as to the quality of stock.

Apart from one or two pre-war importations Arab horses did not begin to come into New Zealand in any number until after the First World War. The New Zealand Arab Breeders Society was set up in 1970 and some little time afterwards the first stud book was published.

In the early days most of the horses came from Australia which is still the largest supplier. Waimeha was the first stud of importance, and the largest up to 1988, when it was dispersed. It was established by the late Alan Sisam, and his mare Gypsy Maid (Sirdar ex Salome), imported from Jos Jelbart's stud in Australia, founded a large family which considerably influenced the breed throughout the country.

Several horses bred by Mrs Dora Maclean at Fenwick, in Australia, were amongst those imported, Sindh being well represented by several sons and daughters. A stallion bred at Crabbet, Silver Sparkle (Oran ex Silver Fire) finally arrived in New Zealand and other British-bred horses include Nurmana (Manak ex Nuhra), bred by Sir Henry and Lady May Abel-Smith, and Ghanimeh (Grey Owl ex Risira) from Mrs E. M. Murray.

Three sons represent the well-known Australian stallion Banderol; Hadban Enzahi, the Egyptian-bred Marbach stallion, also has two sons in New Zealand. More recently Arabians from the USA have been imported including the good stallion Gai Cadet from Gainey Arabains.

With owners of Arabian, Anglo-Arab and partbred horses widely spread through the two islands, local clubs have been formed to organise shows, trail rides and many other activities to keep enthusiasts in touch with each other. Endurance events are especially popular and a National Ride is amongst the new activities being planned.

United States of America

The stud book of the Arabian Horse Registry of the USA has recorded far more registrations than that of any other country – over 400,000 *in toto*. By 1950, however, US registrations were only approaching a total of 5,000 and, as was the case with most other countries, the boom years of such remarkable increase were the 1960s. Though space forbids mention of more than a few of the most important early studs, the contribution of smaller breeders should never be underestimated in countries that are not dominated by state studs.

The founding stallion of Arab horse breeding in the USA was the desert-bred Leopard, imported in 1878 as a gift to President Grant from the Turkish Sultan, Abdul Hamid II. Leopard was acquired by Randolph Huntington, a visionary breeder who tried to create a breed of 'Americo Arabs' using imported Arabians on descendants of a Thoroughbred stallion he had admired many years earlier.

In 1888 Huntington imported Naomi from the Rev. Vidal in England, and her colt by Leopard, foaled in 1891, was the first Arabian bred in North America still represented by registered descent; Naomi was a prolific brood mare and she founded a large family in the USA.

The next step in the early history of Arabians in the New World came when Abdul Hamid authorised a presentation of 'Bedouin Life and Horsemanship' at the Chicago World's Fair in 1893. The Hamidie Hippodrome Company brought 45 horses for the 'Wild East Show' but obligations to return them to their desert homeland were not fulfilled and five of these Arabians appear in the pedigrees of modern descendants.

Between 1898 and 1911 Spencer Borden of Massachusetts imported a number of Arabians from Miss Dillon and the Blunts, including the important mares Rose of Sharon and Ghazala, to his Interlachen Stud. However, it was the political

Rehal, a grandson of Rosa Rugosa, who was by Imamzada (exported to the USA in 1905) out of Rose of Sharon (exported 1906). An important early sire in the USA.

cartoonist, Homer Davenport of New Jersey, who made the largest contribution to early breeding.

Davenport's sense of humour had amused the Blunts when he visited them in 1910 while in England as a correspondent of the *New York World*. His first contact with them had been in 1904 when he sent an agent, Geer, to acquire stock and suggested exchange rather than purchase, wishing to give Angora goats and trotting horses for three Crabbet fillies.

Davenport's enthusiasm for the breed had been fired by the Hamidie Show in Chicago and in 1906 he made a journey to Arabia, the results of which had a profound effect on American Arabian breeding. Travelling to the horse-breeding tribes in their winter quarters he purchased from them 27 stallions and mares, at least 20 of which have bred on into modern pedigrees. Amongst them Hamrah, Deyr and Muson left strong male lines, while the mares Wadduda, Urfah and Werdi were also influential. Davenport acquired other imported horses, including Ibn Mahruss and Abu Zeyd of British breeding. On his early death most of his horses went to Peter Bradley, a financial backer of Davenport's desert expedition, and the main influence of the Davenport horses survived through Bradley's Hingham Stock Farm.

The successor to Spencer Borden's Interlachen Stud was the Maynesboro Stud in New Hampshire, owned by W. R. Brown, a President of the Arabian Horse Club of America and author of *The Horse of the Desert*. The influence of such horses as Rodan, Abu Zeyd, Astraled, Ghazi, Bazrah, Bazleyd and Gulastra comes through Arabians bred at Maynesboro. Brown's own imports from Crabbet dating from 1918 included Berk and the mares Rokhsa, Battla, Simawa and Hazna. Later he added Arabians from France in 1921 and from Egypt in 1932, the latter importations being important through Nasr, Zarife, Roda, Aziza and Mohammed Ali's Hamida.

In 1924 one of the best known American equine 'institutions' of the interwar period came into being: the Kellogg Arabian Horse Ranch. Will K. Kellogg and his brother had established a food company in the 1890s, which proved so successful that by 1906 Will had started up his own company which rapidly became the largest breakfast cereal manufacturer in the country. By 1925 the newspapers were describing him as a multi millionaire.

A chance visit to Southern California brought Kellogg into contact with Carl Schmidt, a German with a life-long passion for Arabians. Kellogg and his friend happened to visit the Arabian stud belonging to Mr C. D. Clarke, and were shown

Abu Zeyd (1904), registered as Lal-i-Abdar in England, by Mesaoud ex Rose Diamond. Exported by his breeder, the Hon. George Savile, to the USA where he was later acquired by Homer Davenport and became one of the most important sires of his time.

round by Schmidt who was in charge of his horses. Carl Schmidt had lived in the Middle East as a young man and he later recorded somewhat fancifully in his travel books his experiences in Arabia. Later books included *The Raswan Index*, an extensive work but questionable as to accuracy and with few references. Some of his theories regarding Arab horse breeding subsequently sparked off controversial reaction from other writers. He was a man of great charm, an idealist whose romantic visions often ran away with him; he was also quick to grasp opportunities for advancing his passion for Arabians.

The wealthy Kellogg asked Schmidt to enquire from Mr Clarke as to whether stock might be for sale. A month later Kellogg found himself the owner of the Clarke horses together with the 'assistance and co-operation of Carl Schmidt', who soon began theorising on the breeding of Arabians and urging development of a large establishment. A ranch was purchased at Pomona, in Southern California, and the horses, nearly all of which had originally come from the Hingham Stud and were thus of Davenport blood-lines, were installed on Schmidt's advice.

Schmidt had great ideas, not only on publicity for the horses (Rudolf Valentino wanted to ride the stallion Jadaan in his next film) but also on further acquisitions; he applied for membership of the British Arab Horse Society for himself and Kellogg and enthusiastically urged a trip to Arabia.

A long eventful saga followed this first flowering of the Kellogg Arabians. Schmidt travelled to England and as a result of his visits to Crabbet a number of horses were purchased by Kellogg from Lady Wentworth, amongst them the stallions Raseyn, Nasik and Ferdin, and the mares Ferda, Farasin, Rifla, Rossana, Incoronata, Crabbet Sura and Rissletta, all of which became very important in the USA.

One of the stallions negotiated for by Schmidt from Lady Wentworth was Raswan, a grey stallion by Skowronek out of Rim, and his arrival at Pomona was to cause the break-up of the Schmidt-Kellogg relationship. The stallion was badly injured in an accident when in Schmidt's care, ending with the death of the horse, the departure of Schmidt from Pomona and his change of name – thereafter Schmidt was known as Carl Raswan.

A new manager, H. Reese, was appointed and under him the Kellogg Arabians flourished. More horses were bought, amongst them a number of W. R. Brown's breeding. With its superb house and stud buildings Pomona was the ideal setting for entertaining and demonstrations; Sunday shows became a feature and were excellent promotion for the breed.

Kellogg had always wanted to make some arrangement whereby Pomona would remain a permanent establishment for breeding Arab horses. He formed an endowment fund, and in 1932 the ranch came under the management of the State of California. During the Second World War Pomona became an Army Remount Depot; when the Americans captured the German State Stud at Hostau and took over the horses as 'prizes of war' it was to Pomona that the Arabians were sent. The horses had been captured by the Germans from Poland, France, Yugoslavia and Hungary and amongst them were Lotnik, Witez II, Chloe, Wierna and Iwonka II. These Polish-bred horses constituted the beginning of the post-war interest in the Polish blood-lines which became a feature of Arab horse breeding in the USA during the 1960s.

Pomona as an establishment ceased to be a remount depot in 1949 when it passed by deed to the Department of Agriculture and became the California State Polytechnic College (Cal Poly) Kellogg Unit.

Three other prominent breeders in the USA before the Second World War who should be mentioned are Roger Selby, General J. M. Dickinson and Henry Babson. The Selby Stud in Ohio has had a profound influence in the USA through such horses as Mirage, Raffles, and Selmian, and the mares Rifala, Indaia, Kareyma, Rose of France and Selmnab, imported from Crabbet in the late 1920s.

General Dickinson established a stud at Traveler's Rest in Tennessee at about the same time with Arabians from Poland, Syria, South America and England. Nasr, Bazleyd, Gulastra, Rose of Luzon, Binni and Gutne are a few of the best-known Traveler's Rest Arabians.

Henry Babson imported five fine horses from Egypt in 1932, including the important stallion Fadl. The 'Babson Egyptians', as they are known, were bred extensively amongst themselves and a large group of them exist today.

A stud which has been in existence for half a century is Al-Marah, owned by Mrs Bazy Tankersley. She started with the purchase in 1942 of Selfra, a mare of Crabbet breeding, and four years later acquired the stallion Indraff (Raffles ex Indaia). Shortly after Lady Wentworth's death in 1957, Mrs Tankersley began negotiations to buy what was the largest consignment of Arabians ever exported from England to the USA. Thirty-two horses were purchased from the Crabbet and Hanstead Studs and shipped to Al-Marah Arabians. Al-Marah, now located in Arizona, is still one of the major studs in the country.

The Gainey Foundation is a stud contemporary with Al-Marah. During the Second World War Daniel C. Gainey was presented by his company with an Arabian colt. A decade later he began his stud in earnest with the acquisition of horses from Albert Harris (who had Crabbet and desert-bred stock) and Roger Selby. The Selby horses were of Crabbet descent with the added blood of Mirage, the desert-bred stallion who spent some years at Crabbet before his exportation to the USA. Gainey later purchased Ferzon and this stallion and the mare Gajala (of

76

Mrs Bazy Tankersley's AM Canadian Beau (1967) by Ranix out of the Indraff daughter, Al-Marah Caliope.

Selby breeding) were the principal foundation horses of the stud. Gainey tried most of the major blood-lines but he quickly eliminated from his stud any which were not successful. Today the Gainey Foundation is run by his son, Daniel J. Gainey, and is basically of Crabbet blood-lines, with some Polish blood.

Thus the foundation animals of the USA came from England and from Arabia itself. Horses descended from these early foundation lines have become known as 'domestic' Arabians and there are many studs which concentrate on breeding

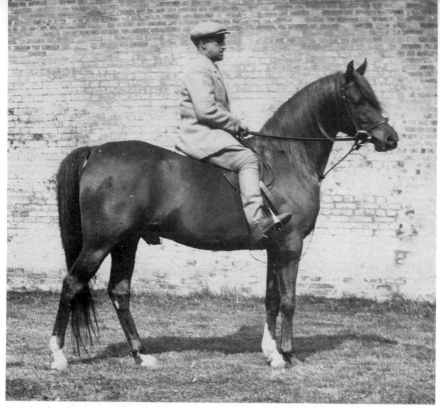

Serafix, by Raktha ex Serafina, at Crabbet, ridden by Fred Rice. He was bought by John Rogers for exportation to the USA as a four year old. Serafix has an exceptional record in the USA and for many years was the leading sire of champions.

horses exclusively from these lines. No mixing has been carried out with recent importations from other countries with assorted blood-lines in their pedigrees. Charles and Jeanne Craver have kept a unique collection of Arabians descended solely from Davenport horses at their stud in Illinois. One of the leading sires in the USA, and a great show winner in the 1970s, is Khemosabi (Amerigo ex Jurneeka), whose pedigree includes 'Babson Egyptian' and Polish horses but mostly 'old' blood-lines.

As the 1970s boom gathered momentum, however, breeders in the USA began importing horses from various other countries, frequently paying enormous prices for them. 'Modern Egyptian' Arab horses (as opposed to the 'Old Egyptians' bred from pre-First World War horses) became popular. Mr and Mrs Douglas Marshall were amongst the earlier importers and one of the principal stallions at their Gleannloch Farms in Texas was Morafic (Nazeer ex Mabrouka). Judith and Don Forbis were other early importers and their Ansata Arabian stud in Oklahoma is amongst the foremost stud farms specialising in horses of Egyptian blood-lines.

Khemosabi (1967) by Amerigo ex Jurneeka, bred by Mr and Mrs B. P. Husband – the USA and Canadian National Champion and leading living sire of national champions.

Arabians of Polish blood-lines were likewise much sought after and a number of studs were founded with these importations; they were also incorporated into existing studs to cross with 'domestic' stock. Notable sires included Bask (Witraz ex Balalajka) and Nabor (Negativ ex Lagodna), both of which had a colossal influence on American breeding.

Later it was Russian-bred horses which became fashionable, though it should be explained that many of the pedigrees of Polish and Russian Arabians include the same horses due to the interchanges of stock during and after the Second World War. Also, mainly through the sale of the Crabbet Stud consignment to the USSR in 1936, a large number of Russian-bred Arabians carry quite a high percentage of English blood.

Prominent amongst stallions of Russian blood-lines are Muscat (Salon ex Malpia) and Nariadni (Nabeg ex Nariadnaia), but it is still too early to measure the lasting value of recently imported individual animals to American Arab horse breeding as a whole.

Space forbids description here of the many large American studs which have achieved prominence in the 1970s and 1980s. A number in fact have gone out of business. The boom swelled to giant bubble proportions and of course eventually burst. Studs which had been producing a hundred or more foals each year suddenly found that the hyped-up auction sales at which they had been selling comparatively few horses each year – but at astronomical prices to enable them to stay in business – were failing. The bottom had dropped out of the market.

On the credit side there have been many large breeders who have aimed to produce the finest Arabians without running their studs solely for commercial success. Most are continuing to breed, but on a reduced scale. Stallion report statistics show a significant drop in the number of mares covered each year from well over 47,000 in 1985 to 31,000 in 1989.

In the meantime there are a great many dedicated smaller breeders who feel that in the long term a reduction in the number of very large 'showing' studs could prove to be of overall benefit to the breed. They believe that the true versatile Arabian, divorced from the hype and artificiality of extreme showing practices, will continue to gain admirers and prove increasingly popular as an all-round performance horse.

South America

South America has a very large population of Arabians. Some are bred to produce good quality half-breds and working horses for the large cattle ranches. Many are now bred for sport and showing as in Europe and the USA. Horses were imported to Argentina from the Middle East and elsewhere in the nineteenth century, and importation has continued to the present day. Brazil's Arab horse numbers grew dramatically with heavy importation in the 1980s. The countries of South America have nevertheless developed their breeding somewhat in isolation from the rest of the world. Mexico, which has a growing nucleus of breeders, and the United States are most open to South American influence.

South Africa

The first horses of Arabian origin to arrive in South Africa went there from the Far East in the seventeenth century. Arab traders took horses to Java in the late fourteenth and fifteenth centuries and it was the descendants of these animals which were imported into South Africa.

They were followed by Persian horses and then by some from South America which were descendants of Arabians and Barbs. Between 1795 and 1860 a few horses of Arabian breeding were imported from India. All these early horses contributed to the Cape Horse and the founding of the 'Boerperd'.

The South African Stud Book was established by the Government in 1905 and the first Arab entries were made in 1908. These early horses were largely from Crabbet stock but practically all trace of them has been lost, except for one known mare line.

The commencement of purebred Arab breeding dates from 1938 when Mr C. E. Orpen, a great horse breeder, imported from England the stallion Jiddan, of mostly Crabbet breeding. He later instigated the purchase of six Arabians from Egypt. Since neither King Farouk nor the Egyptian Agricultural Organisation wanted to sell to individuals these horses were bought by the South African Government and transferred to private owners after their arrival.

In 1946 Mr G. C. Kock imported three stallions and two mares of Crabbet breeding, but his stud was dispersed in 1951. However, by this time interest in breeding purebred Arabians was gathering momentum; between 1945 and 1958 around 60 horses were imported from Britain and a few from the USA, to form the true foundation of South African Arabian stock.

One of the most important of the earlier Arabians exported from Britain to South Africa was Raktha (Naseem ex Razina). He was bred at Hanstead but

81

acquired by Lady Wentworth when young and spent most of his life at Crabbet. Raktha was 16 when he went abroad in 1951 but nevertheless exerted considerable influence in South Africa as a sire.

Arabians bred at Hanstead also formed the main foundation stock of Mr and Mrs J. Grobbelaar's Jamani Stud. They imported their first mare, Correze (Count Dorsaz ex Namilla), in 1955; later she was joined by Garance (Grey Owl ex Rikitea) and Zena (Blue Domino ex Queen Zenobia) and the stallion Grantchester (General Grant ex Rafeena). Jamani has been one of the most important studs in South Africa and all the above horses have had a great influence on Arab horse breeding in the country. Grantchester also won in-hand and under saddle at major shows, and countless show champions descend from Jamani horses. The Jamani Stud, in the ownership of Charmaine Grobbelaar since her husband died some

Mrs Charmaine Grobbelaar with Grantchester (1952), Supreme Champion purebred in South Africa, 1963. Bred at Hanstead, he was by General Grant out of Rafeena.

Raktha Sadha, by Royal Crystal (Dargee ex Grey Royal by Raktha) out of Rosina, ridden by Miss V. Hankey in 1971. She came fourth in a point-to-point at a Cape Hunt and Polo Club race meeting in South Africa against Thoroughbreds.

years ago, has recently been revived by amalgamation with the horses belonging to Mrs Grobbelaar's cousin, Leonard Buys.

Mr and Mrs John Kettlewell started their Jericho Stud in 1951, their foundation mare being the British-bred Fayalina (Fayal ex Naama) and her filly Irexia by Irex. In 1970 the colt Barabaz (Stargard ex Razalana) was purchased in England and he proved a very successful stud sire. During the 1970s interest grew in horses of Egyptian breeding and the Kettlewells imported Omar El Shaker, bred by Om El Arab Stud in Germany. Later, in 1985, they added Nafal, by the Russian Nadejni out of the Polish mare, Flanka.

The Vidiko Stud, belonging to the Voorendyk family, imported Darius (Ghazal ex Darsi) of Egyptian/Marbach ancestry. The German-bred El Shaklan is represented by his son, Niyashan el Shaklan, while Juan, by Lavado, was imported from Spain, these last two in different ownership.

These are just a few of the studs and horses which are prominent in South African breeding but they are representative of the current trend. While some breeders have introduced an infusion of Egyptian, Spanish and Polish or Russian blood, few breeders are breeding exclusively from these 'new' imports; but there are a number who are breeding solely from the 'old' English stock.

An interesting innovation is 'The 500 Challenge', an event designed to find the best all-round Arabian horse, first staged at the 1990 Natal Regional Show. The class was judged in three phases, in-hand, as a riding horse, and utility and jumping. The South Africans place considerable importance on ridden classes at shows and many of their top in-hand winners have been equally successful under saddle.

Canada

There were very few purebred Arabians in Canada before the Second World War and those which did come into the country were often used only for cross-breeding. After the war a few studs were formed, the original stock having come almost entirely from Britain and the USA.

At that time there was still a prejudice against the breed but, as in other countries, it was often one or two individual horses which did most to dispel the common misconception that Arabians cannot jump or are no good as performance horses.

One such ambassador for the breed was Ferishal, a 14.3 h.h. stallion by Ferhal, out of Rishafieh, who was exported from England to the USA where she produced Ferishal. He went as a foal to Mrs Trethewey in British Columbia and when his training began at three years old he soon displayed his potential as a brilliant all-round performer. The highlight of his career came in 1962 when, at the age of 13, he was selected to join the San Fernando Rey Team for the famous Three-Day Event at Pebble Beach, California. Miss Helen Howe, reporting the event in *The Arabian Horse World*, wrote: 'An Arab named Ferishal came down to do a tremendous job for the breed! I cannot tell you what an impression this little horse made on the spectators. People I know as detractors of the Arab were all exclaiming over him.'

Canada now has a large number of studs, many of which were started with Arabians from the USA. One breeder who is concentrating on producing performance horses for a variety of events is Mr F. Hanneschlager, who has a stud founded with horses of Davenport (American) breeding. Mr Hanneschlager has trained some of his Arabians for driving and they have become well known in British Columbia for the superb performances they give in harness competing against all other breeds.

Egypt

Arabians have been bred in Egypt for a very long time and, as we have seen, the Abbas Pasha collection has been by far the greatest influence on the breed.

When Ali Pasha Sherif's stud was dispersed at the end of the nineteenth century his horses were acquired largely by Lady Anne Blunt and a group of Egyptian breeders, commonly referred to as 'the Princes' – sons of Ali Pasha Sherif and others of high rank.

The collection of Prince Kemal el Dine Hussein formed the Inshass Royal Stud, which was later owned by the kings of Egypt. When King Farouk was dethroned in 1952 the horses were confiscated and incorporated into the Government stud.

In 1892 the Egyptian Government had founded a Horse Commission to obtain horses for the police and army. The Commission was merged with the breeding section of the Royal Agricultural Society of Egypt (RAS) in 1908 and two stud farms were acquired near Cairo. The Government had difficulty in obtaining good sires and for some years used English Thoroughbreds on their mares. Progeny, however, was unsatisfactory and in 1914 the decision was made to breed only purebred Arabians.

Over the next few years 16 mares and 48 stallions were bought or given as gifts to form the foundation stock of the stud. Some of the horses were of Ali Pasha Sherif blood-lines but the Egyptians wanted more Arabians of this breeding and turned to England where one of the largest concentrations of Ali Pasha Sherif blood was to be found in the Crabbet Stud. In 1920 negotiations were concluded for the purchase of 16 stallions and a filly from Lady Wentworth as breeding stock for the RAS studs.

In 1952 the RAS was renamed the Egyptian Agricultural Organisation (EAO). Their El Zahraa Stud at Ein Shems, near Cairo, under the direction (from 1960 for nearly thirty years) of Dr Mohamed Marsafi, has had a great influence on Arab horse breeding throughout the world and amongst the earlier important horses bred in Egypt one or two stand out as being exceptional. Undoubtedly one of the greatest was Nazeer. He was by Mansour out of Bint Samiha, a daughter of Kazmeen who, with his sire Sotamm, was included in the group purchased from the Crabbet Stud. Nazeer's sons have spread his influence throughout the world, notably Morafic, Ibn Halima, Talal and Fakher el Din in the USA, the great Aswan in the USSR and Hadban Enzahi, Kaisoon and Ghazal in Germany. Equally important amongst many others are the daughters of Nazeer, Bint Moniet el Nefous and Bint Mabrouka (whose dams were both outstanding mares), Bint Bukra and Bint Zaafarana. A son of Moniet el Nefous, Ibn Moniet el Nefous, was another great sire.

During the 1960s and 1970s many of the best horses at El Zahraa were purchased for large figures by American breeders. This somewhat depleted the stud which has gone through difficult times, but it is still of great importance. There are also a few private studs in Egypt, the best known being that belonging to Madame el Barbary, which is situated near the Pyramids.

Jordan

Finally in this brief discourse on the Arab scene throughout the world mention must be made of the Royal Stud of Jordan, one of the most important in the Middle East.

A group of mares at the Royal Stud of Jordan.

Sheroule, by Bahar out of Sabal II, a mare of the Royal Stud of Jordan.

The original stock was descended from horses owned by King Abdullah, grandfather of King Hussein, the present ruler; all female lines trace directly to the desert, as do some of the sire lines. Over the years other horses have been added to the stud from Spain, Egypt and Iraq and more recently from Britain.

The high standard of the stock bred at the Royal Stud is due in no small measure to the enthusiasm and expertise of the king's daughter, Princess Alia al Hussein. A much respected judge and expert on the breed, the princess initiated the first inter-Arabian Show, held in Jordan in 1988. It was a unique occasion enjoyed by Arab horse admirers from many countries around the world. As Princess Alia wrote: 'It is always a pleasure to note how the Arabian has the ability to bring together in a positive way people of different cultures and ideologies.'

5 Characteristics and use

Description

The classic Arabian horse strikes the eye immediately with its beauty and symmetry, and it should be remembered that the latter quality, together with natural good balance, is closely allied to efficient movement. The Thoroughbred, having evolved mainly from horses of Eastern blood, is often compared with the Arabian and certainly surpasses it for speed but in temper, vitality, soundness and general utility the Arabian is far superior.

The Arabs themselves valued three chief characteristics above all others: the head, the curve of the throat (mitbah) and the high carriage of the tail. The head is important, and in fineness should proclaim the true high-caste Arabian; any coarseness here is a fault. The setting of the eyes is distinctive to the breed, being lower in the head than others, with prominent eye-socket and finely chiselled bone. The forehead should be broad, the jowl deep, and the head should taper to a small muzzle. The eye should be large and dark; white showing at the corners is not uncommon and is no fault; it is set into the head at a different angle to most breeds and is round compared to the more triangular eye-shape of 'cold-blooded' horses.

Stallions should have small beautifully shaped ears, the tips sharply defined and sometimes turning inwards slightly. Mares often have larger ears but they should be equally finely cut. Hearing is acute, the ears are often pricked and alertness is much apparent in the quick individual ear movements. Large slack ears are a fault.

The nostrils, which have a greater capacity for expansion than in any other breed, should be large, delicate and finely carved. The mouth is long, with the lips close and firm, the bars of the mouth being particularly long.

Although a straight profile, especially in stallions, is not a fault the ideal is a slight dipping below the eyes to give a concave curve. But the concavity should not be too high up, thereby giving an over-prominent forehead, nor should it be so deep that it results in a curve over the nose.

Facial expression is important. It should be gentle but eloquent and sparkling in a mare, while the eyes of stallions when aroused may fairly blaze with exuberance. The skin is dark and the eyelashes long.

The jowl should be well defined, with good width between the cheek-bones. The set-on of head is most important, for it gives the beautiful curve of throat-line which

89

is one of the most distinguishing features of the Arabian. The neck should be long, gently curved in a mare while stallions have a distinctive crest. The top of the neck behind the ears is well muscled, and the neck should be arched in a curve from this point to the withers, which should be high and well defined and spring back from the neck. It is a fault should the neck underline be too protrusive when the head is held high.

The shoulder should be long, well-sloped and very free in movement. If the shoulder blade is set too upright the foreleg cannot swing forward properly, so restricting the stride. Forelegs should be straight, with powerful forearm, big flat knees and short cannon bones, the tendons clearly defined. The Arabian has much greater density of bone than other breeds and a large measurement below the knee is not necessary as long as the back tendons are not tied in below the knee. The pasterns should be reasonably long and may slope more than other breeds. The feet should be hard and smooth, of fair size and rounded in shape, especially the forefeet. Small narrow feet are bad, as are large or shallow ones; a club foot is also a fault.

Arabians have five lumbar vertebrae instead of six and generally have 17 ribs, against the 18 or 19 of other breeds, and are therefore shorter in the back. The tail should be set-on very high and gaily raised when its owner is in motion; some arch their tails even when standing alert. High tail carriage denotes a strong back and the ability to carry great weight for size.

The chest should be broad, the girth deep and the ribs well rounded; there should be a 'leg at each corner', as the saying goes. In older animals, especially brood mares, the appearance of a dipped-back, or saddle-back, is sometimes due to especially prominent withers and is not necessarily a weakness. Any sinking in front of the hips or weakness in the loins, however, is a fault.

The quarters should be much more level than in other breeds; short or sloping quarters are bad. Photographs of desert-bred Arabians, and of the early mares in studs all over the world, frequently show a prominence of the croup (often described as a 'jumping bump') usually combined with a noticeably high tail setting; this should not be considered a fault. The ideal is a comparatively level back, shaped in gentle curves and with 'somewhere to put the saddle'. The straight so-called 'table-top' back is not correct and may indicate weakness or stiff movement, giving a poor ride.

The Arabian is exceptionally long from the hip and stifle to hocks, thereby tending to give an appearance of having more angle to the hock than other breeds.

Artist's impression of the Arabian horse.

The hocks therefore are well let down and accordingly the thighs and gaskins should be muscular and strong; any weakness here is bad. Hocks should be large and should not turn inwards.

The true Arabian action is distinctive; it should be light and springy, powerful apparently without effort. When walking there is free shoulder movement and when moving fast the hind feet should overstep the front footmarks by about a foot. Trotting action is very free, the forelegs darting out from the shoulders with the feet seeming to dwell momentarily in the air – a suspended yet floating movement. The hock action should be powerful, with the hocks brought forward in a swinging stride. Often when trotting fast an Arabian will go rather wide behind. High knee action and trailing hocks are both bad.

Usual colours are chestnut, bay or grey; very dark brown or black are rare. Young grey horses can vary considerably from a light rose grey to dark steel or dappled, and many become fleabitten with age. Chestnuts, and sometimes bays, often have a large white marking on the head and white legs but this is no defect;

91

many of the best Arabians carried much white. Colour and markings should be secondary considerations to type and quality.

There is no height limit. Arabians can vary from less than 14 h.h. to nearly 16 h.h., averaging between 14.2 h.h. and 15 h.h.

The general impression of an Arabian should be of a horse of great quality, striking appearance, and proud bearing. Quality is particularly apparent in the silkiness of coat, mane and tail, and in fine bone structure.

Strains and types

The myths and fables surrounding the origins of the Arabian breed give rise to various theories regarding strains. The word 'type' can lead to misunderstanding as it has two meanings: certain writers have used it to delineate original desert strains or families; in current language, the word 'type' or 'typy' is often used to describe the degree of beauty or Arabian characteristics in an individual.

The myth attributing five (seven has sometimes been quoted) principal strains to the favourite mares of the Prophet (or Salaman, descendant of Ishmael, or even Solomon – writers do not agree on the original owner) is, according to Lady Anne Blunt, of comparatively modern origin, authorised by no tradition: indeed, the names given to these five strains are frequently different. The theory promoted by Carl Raswan of there being three, not five, main strains is further confused when these three strains are designated 'types': Kehilan (said to be of masculine type symbolising power and endurance), Seglawi (feminine and symbol of beauty and elegance) and Muniqi (angular and rangy, for speed). Raswan maintained that the Arabs classified their horses in this way but Lady Wentworth strongly repudiated his claim. Lady Anne Blunt never made any mention of the Arabs believing in three distinct strains or types; she listed many strains and sub-strains existing in the desert, all valued by Arabs. It would appear that the 'three type' theory could be of Western origin since knowledgeable Arabs are known to dismiss it.

The generic term given to Arabians is Kehilan Ajuz, meaning the thoroughbred, or purebred, horse of antiquity. In Arab horses the strain (or family) name is always taken from the mare. Certain mares or families became famous for prowess in warfare and often went by the names of their owners; others were given a name from a district. From several original strain names sub-strains were formed, and phonetic spellings of the words differ; also mare and stallion strain names always have a different ending.

Since the Arabs often bred their horses 'pure within the strain' it is conceivable that inherited likenesses tended to stabilise in some families, and led to certain differences in appearance between various strains. Certainly there has always been a variation in type of horses in Arabia, within the breed characteristics.

Arab horses which have been bred outside Arabia for many generations are seldom bred 'within the strain' and if an analysis was made of modern pedigrees the majority of Arabians would be found to contain a mixture of strains in their pedigrees. However, as in all animal breeding, in addition to family likenesses developing, certain breeders will tend to produce a 'type' of Arabian which they personally admire most. This applies to state as well as private studs and can explain remarks such as 'Polish type', or 'Russian look', often heard these days, in the same manner that the aforementioned 'Clark type', for example, emerged. Differences will of course exist, but the overriding qualities, basic conformation and characteristics already described should be inherent in all top-class Arabians.

Problems of the breed

The Arabian is very intelligent and has a lively disposition, and it must be said that they are not always ideal for certain people. On the other hand one so often hears of others who, once they have owned or ridden an Arabian, say they could never go back to another breed. It all depends on the individual, and Arabians can be made or marred by their trainer like any other horse.

Being high spirited and energetic they do not take kindly to a life of being shut in stables most of the day. They enjoy being out and about and joining in with whatever is happening in their home. One has only to watch youngsters in their paddock taking a keen interest in everything that humans do around the place to realise that Arabians profit enormously from human companionship. Having been for centuries brought up in close proximity with man this trait is hardly surprising. Owners who do not fully appreciate this are likely to miss out on some of the enjoyment of having Arabians.

Being a small compact horse it does not necessarily suit riders wanting size and scope, but what the Arabian lacks in inches it makes up for in strength. The true Arab action, which is light and springy, gives the feeling that one could ride all day with pleasure and comfort.

Some dressage experts complain that the Arabian's short back and general conformation make it unsuitable for this particular discipline. It tends to be less supple than some other horses. There is the fallacy that it cannot jump and dislikes going through water. This may be true of certain individuals – one can never generalise in any breed – but many Arabians are excellent jumpers and show great courage when it comes to tackling fences designed for horses of 16 h.h. or more.

A problem known to the Arabian horse is CID (Combined Immunodeficiency Disease). Since it is probably hereditary it could have existed undiscovered for an indeterminable length of time and although research is continuing there is so far no test capable of identifying carriers. Foals with this disease usually die before they are 6 months old, normally from less serious illnesses such as pneumonia, because their systems cannot make antibodies. Of course, it is very sad for a breeder to lose a foal in this way but the number of fatalities is relatively small compared to other causes of foal deaths and if one is unfortunate enough to have a foal with CID one would obviously not repeat the same mating, since the disease only occurs if both parents are carriers. When a carrier test becomes available it will be an easy matter to avoid matings between carriers and theoretically it should then be possible to control the disease strictly and even eventually to eliminate it.

Although Arabians are thin-skinned and do not grow very heavy winter coats they are comparatively hardy. They do not need as much concentrated feed as Thoroughbreds – in fact, care has to be taken that they do not suffer from laminitis should they be kept on too much rich grass, become over-fat, or have insufficient exercise. This is not to say that they should be underfed, or left to fend for themselves – no youngsters will grow up strong and healthy if care is not applied to their diet. Nor will they do well if insufficiently exercised during early growth. A small enclosed paddock, where the mare can graze, is the ideal place for a newly born foal to run out for short periods. At first they should be brought into their loose-box for sleeping periods during the day if the weather is not warm, and of course at nights. After a week or so they can join other mares with foals and at two months old, if the weather is neither cold nor wet, they can stay out all day and even at night if it is summertime.

By then they should be in large paddocks. Nothing is better for growing foals and youngstock than to have plenty of space for playing and galloping; the mares enjoy it too. The practice of highly feeding young horses to 'boost' them for the show ring, keeping them boxed year-round, with insufficient exercise, is artificial and injurious. It can result in problems connected with bone development, and Arabians reared in this way can suffer leg troubles, virtually unknown to those reared in the proper way. The desert-reared Arabian had very good lungs, due to its outdoor life; if there is any lung weakness in stable-reared horses the trouble is largely due to incorrect management. Stables should be airy but not draughty, and care should be taken to see that both bedding and, even more important, hay is clean and dust-free.

Youngsters need shelter and warmth in the winter, and they particularly dislike wet, windy weather. Stabled at night and out all day is the best treatment – they even enjoy a roll in snow! Mares which are not in foal do very well out all the time, always provided the climate is not extreme, but a good shelter is essential in which they can keep warm and dry in rainy weather, and they must be given adequate food.

In the same way stallions are much more contented if kept in paddocks with a stable attached in which they will soon learn to shelter against winter weather or summer flies. They benefit from plenty of exercise and enjoy being ridden; it keeps them fit and virile. There was a lot to be said for the 'old' practice of walking stallions great distances each day to cover mares. Walking, preferably including a hill or two, is highly beneficial – there is nothing like it for stallions and youngstock for promoting fitness and muscular development. This also applies to show horses; a well-muscled, hard-looking youngster is more impressive than the flabby over-fat animal too often seen today. Fat can conceal a multitude of faults – breeders and owners should give priority to rearing strong healthy horses.

Ample good grazing in summer, high-quality hay in winter and sufficient hard feed (ensuring that correct mineral balance is taken) will keep Arabians fit and well. Soil conditions vary so much according to locality that there is no hard and fast rule regarding any mineral deficiencies which may need rectifying. Arabians are no different to other breeds inasmuch as commonsense and a sound knowledge of general care are needed to ensure happy, healthy stock.

Training

It has already been stressed that Arabians are highly intelligent. It was once said by someone who had successfully trained purebreds, Anglo-Arabs and partbreds for a variety of disciplines that 'the trouble with Arabs is that they are too damned clever!'

They learn quickly and can easily get bored by recurring exercises – the lesson learnt, they can see no point in continuous repetition! Similarly, Arabians being trained for racing thrive on variety of route when on daily exercise.

The basic teaching which all young horses should have from foalhood onwards applies to Arabians, bearing in mind that lessons are learnt extra quickly. Even with older horses if training lapses for several months Arabians usually carry on from where it was left off, for they have long memories. It has been known for older brood mares which have been well handled all their lives to be ridden bareback with little or no training.

People unfamiliar with Arabian stallions sometimes consider them as 'fiery' or 'peacocky'. To do so is not to appreciate the natural presence and gaiety of the breed, and mistakenly equate it with a temperament difficult to handle. It is true that many stallions are high-spirited and those who seek to train them with roughness or by abuse will end up with problems. No horse should be treated roughly and the more intelligent, courageous and sensitive the animal the more should its training be appropriate to these qualities.

Arabian stallions are often especially gentle with children; they will dance around in high spirits when handled by an adult, but walk quietly if led by a child. Arabians also seem to know if anyone suffering a disability is handling them. They become especially tractable, and there have been cases of severly disabled riders accomplishing great feats mounted on Arabians.

Role in the desert and uses today

Before the advent of the motor car and modern fighting methods the Arabian was used essentially as a war horse by the Bedouin. It was also a status symbol with the ruling families in the Middle East.

Up to the twentieth century the principal horse-breeding tribes of Arabia owned large numbers of horses and camels. When trekking from one pasture to another the Bedouin rode their camels and either led their mares or allowed them to follow; foals ran loose. Camels were essential for providing milk for mares and foals as well as for humans and they could carry great loads, but the strength of a tribe also lay in the number of horsemen it could muster and the prowess of its mounted warriors.

The Bedouin's mare was his most precious possession. Not only was she a necessity for raiding and battle, but her speed could save his life if he was pursued by an enemy; in addition she became his friend and companion. Thus the characteristics of intelligence, speed and endurance were most highly regarded by the Arabs and exceptional mares became famous amongst the tribes for these

A typical versatile Arabian, Rizanna (1979) by Nazir ex El Sain, bred by Miss F. E. Dowse-Brenan. With her owner, Mrs Lynn Cornish, Rizanna has competed successfully in show jumping, hunter trials, dressage and team chasing, as well as being a member of the Courage Ladies' Side-saddle Display Team.

qualities. Stealing of mares was often reason for continuous wars, and disputed ownership of a celebrated mare could also cause deep family feuds.

When fighting, the Arabs carried a lance (which could be as much as 20 feet long in some of the northern tribes) and their mounts had to be extremely agile, able to stop dead in their stride, spin on their hocks and dart off again.

All these characteristics of the breed, together with its undoubted quality and prepotency, have been recognised by breeders for centuries and, as will be seen in Chapter 6, the Arabian has been used to upgrade many types of horse and pony.

Today, in addition to its value for cross-breeding, the Arabian can be trained for all kinds of performance work. Although its height, compared to hunters, show jumpers and eventers, is a drawback for riders preferring a larger horse for this work, Arabians are often hunted and have competed successfully in jumping and eventing. Conversely, their smaller size is more suitable for young people and an increasing number of junior riders are enjoying a wide variety of activities mounted on purebred Arabians. They are extremely versatile and with their natural exuberance, bravery and *joie de vivre* will relish anything from gymkhana events to going across country. They are also driven in harness and trained for circus acts.

The racing of Arab horses is becoming a very popular sport in many countries, but the true metier of the breed is in endurance riding and here it reigns supreme against all breeds.

The Arabian in endurance riding

Endurance feats by Arabians are inherent in their history and it is hardly surprising that they are supreme amongst all breeds in long distance riding. In addition to remarkable staying power they have the courage and generosity to give of their best in this most demanding discipline. In the organised rides of today horses of Arabian breeding are invariably in the forefront and the demand for them as endurance mounts is growing steadily.

During the 1920s when the AHS was holding its 300-mile tests in England, similar events were concurrent in the USA. One Arabian mare, the Crabbet-bred Ramla, carried 14½ stone to victory in a 310-mile race, while the gelding named Crabbet is said to have exceeded this by carrying 17½ stone over the same distance. To carry such weights over long distances exemplifies in addition the Arabian's remarkable strength for its size.

Endurance riding as we know it today first began to develop in the USA during the middle of the twentieth century. The world's most famous endurance ride, the Western States 100 Miles One-Day Ride, was pioneered by Wendell Robie in 1955 to find whether the modern trail horse matched the horses of the nineteenth-century Gold Rush days. This race, over spectacular mountainous country from Nevada to California, has to be completed in 24 hours and it is run under very strict veterinary supervision. Known as the Tevis Cup, from the winner's trophy, it is an annual event and from its inception it has been completely dominated by horses of Arabian breeding - over 90% of the winners being Arabians or their derivatives.

Today two main organisations, for trail and endurance riding, put on literally hundreds of events all over the USA. In 1987 a grey Arabian gelding, Rushcreek

Negotiating the Cougar Rock in the world's most famous endurance ride, the 100 Mile Tevis Cup in the USA. Juliet Moss on Sahara Ace.

Lad, set a record in the USA. He and his owner, Trilby Pederson, a 53-year-old mother of six, in one year completed 73 endurance rides, covering a total of 4,260 miles. Although never actually winning a ride they were AERC (American Endurance Ride Conference) Champions of the year. Mrs Pederson's policy – just to complete the ride, never pushing her horse for a win – paid off since miles, not wins, were championship criteria; some contenders were forced to retire lame, and her victory was said to open up a new concept for the USA in that caring for one's mount during rides proved wiser than an all-out effort to win.

Australia is another leading country in endurance riding and there the great race is the Quilty 100 Miler. It is said to have been started after a chance remark, at a meeting of the Arab Horse Society of Australia, that it was a pity the public were not aware that Australian horses must rank among the best in the world. The famous horseman Tom Quilty presented a handsome gold trophy for the event and the inaugural race held in 1966 was won by Gabriel Stecher who completed the whole course bareback on the Arabian stallion Shalawi. Australian long distance rides are considered amongst the toughest anywhere. Over the last two decades, under the guidance of the Australian Endurance Riders Association, the sport has flourished and produces some of the best riders and horses in the world.

In 1965 the AHS resumed its attempts to foster long-distance riding by holding a ride at Goodwood over a course of 50 miles for Arab or Arab-bred horses carrying a minimum of 11½ stone. That same year the British Horse Society held a ride on Exmoor, also over 50 miles, called the Golden Horseshoe Ride. In 1968 the two societies combined to run their events together at Goodwood. Since then the Golden Horseshoe Ride, with Arab Horse Society help for the first few years, has become an important annual long distance event.

The Endurance Horse and Pony Society of Great Britain (EHPS) began holding rides of various lengths in 1973 and has now established its 100 mile Summer Solstice Ride as one of the highlights of the European long distance riding calendar. In 1974 it started a high points sytem for the leading endurance horse; the winner for the first two years was Ann Hyland's Arabian stallion Nizzolan. Several other purebred stallions have excelled in endurance, including Val Long's Tarim, who was fourth overall in the first World Endurance Riding Championships, held in Rome in 1986, and the highest placed horse in the British team which won.

There are far too many horses of Arab breeding which have made names for themselves in endurance riding to include them all here. Suffice to say that they dominate the long distance riding scene in Britain.

Two Young National Champion Endurance riders in the Golden Horseshoe Ride, 1991.
Claire Brown, the 1989 National Champion, with her purebred mare, Shireen Lailee (1977)
by Paradazy ex Lady Shamrock, bred by Mrs G. Bartlett, leads Nic Wigley at the Tarr Steps
on Exmoor. Nic Wigley with her purebred gelding Marbat (1978) by Haroun ex Mahbubat
Bint El Malik, bred by M. A. Pitt-Rivers, was Junior Champion of 1990 and 1991 and also
won the Belgian Condroz Ride in 1991.

One particularly memorable year was 1990, for the endurance team won
Britain's only gold medal at the World Equestrian Games in Stockholm; this was
the first time endurance riding was included in the programme. Three of the British
horses which finished in the top ten possessed Arabian blood and the fourth is
believed to be an Arab/Welsh cross; the winner of the individual silver medal was
Jane Donovan with her purebred gelding Ibriz.

Janet Robbins and Dundrum Easter Robin, one of the many partbred Arabs which have been so successful in long distance riding.

Of other European countries France has one of the longest histories of endurance riding, although its national body was not founded until 1982. Many of its leading riders have Arabian or partbred horses and French teams are much respected in the international scene.

The overall governing body for endurance riding in Europe, the European Long Distance Rides Conference (ELDRIC), has awarded the ELDRIC Points Trophy annually since 1980. This has become one of the most coveted awards, and British riders have had an excellent record, frequently with purebred Arabian horses.

It can be seen that endurance riding has expanded rapidly over the last two decades. Both this activity and racing test the outstanding qualities of the Arabian – stamina, speed, soundness and courage – and its success in long distance events does much to promote its image.

The Arabian in dressage

The art of high-school riding has been practised for many years on the Continent but at the time when the late Henry Wynmalen was giving demonstrations with his famous Shagya, Basa, dressage was only in its infancy in Britain. Now its importance is fully recognised and many competitions at international level are held all over Europe, and elsewhere.

The first purebred in England to gain recognition at a high level of dressage was Golden Wings (Bright Shadow ex Silent Wings), bred by Mrs E. M. Thomas and owned by the Countess of Pembroke. Golden Wings represented Great Britain in 1980 in Belgium and at Goodwood International Meeting, where he won the prize for the highest placed British entry competing in Prix St George and his rider, Carol Pearce, won the saddle presented to the British rider gaining the most points in three days of competition.

It has to be acknowledged, however, that Anglo-Arabs and partbreds generally produce a superior performance to purebreds. Prince Consort, by the Thoroughbred Regal Boy out of the Anglo mare Scindian Enchantress by Scindian Magic, has already been mentioned as an Anglo-Arab which has reached Olympic standard.

Many other Arabians and their derivatives are now found performing at various levels and, even if they do not all reach the top in competition, they are certainly giving their owners and riders much pleasure. Their graceful and fluid movements are, to many, more attractive to watch than the performances of the somewhat massive larger breeds, whose very size and build often oblige their riders to adopt an active style of riding in order to maintain accuracy.

6 The influence of the Arabian

Arabians have been used for centuries to upgrade different breeds, and as can be seen in Chapters 3 and 4 their influence was particularly strong in Europe. However, the greatest breed to evolve from Eastern horses is the Thoroughbred.

The Thoroughbred

According to Lady Wentworth, the Arab ancients are said to have worshipped a horse god called Ya'uk and in Southern Arabia the idol was Ya'bub (a swift horse). Be that as it may, it is incontrovertible that the source of the hot-blooded 'racing' horses was Arabia.

Chariot racing was one of the earliest forms of the sport and instructions on training horses for this were, also according to Lady Wentworth, given in the Hittite Treatise of Kikkulis, dating from 1360 BC. There are many references to mounted horse races in ancient Arabic works and there is no doubt that speed and endurance were qualities highly prized by early breeders. Lady Wentworth writes of racing in the Kingdom of Hira in AD 120 and of the Prophet, an enthusiastic racehorse owner and admirer of the Arabian, conducting Arab racing around the middle of the sixth century. Horse and camel races are said to have taken place at El Haifa in AD 687.

The Arabian is the swiftest pure old breed of horse. The Thoroughbred and the Quarter Horse, although faster, having been evolved from Oriental sires and mares of mixed breeding, cannot be considered of pure descent compared to the Arabian with its more ancient lineage.

It is an astonishing fact that all Thoroughbreds trace in the male line to just three Eastern stallions, the Darley Arabian, the Godolphin Arabian and the Byerley Turk.

The Byerley Turk

The first of these three to come to England was the Byerley Turk who, according to K. M. Haralambos, arrived at Portsmouth with his owner in 1688. In her book, *The Byerley Turk*, Mrs Haralambos describes how Captain Robert Byerley, together with his independently raised troop of cavalry, had been attached to the Duke of

Lorraine's army and had been fighting against the Turks in Hungary to defend Christendom. They had won a notable victory at Buda and as a spoil of war Captain Byerley had acquired a magnificent dark bay Arabian stallion. The horse became known as 'Byerley's Treasure' and was the envy of the captain's brother officers.

Portraits and descriptions of the horse suggest he was an Arabian, but it is easy to see how he came to be known as the Byerley Turk. In those days the terms Arabian, Barb and Turk were not as clearly defined as they were to become when horses began to be registered in stud books.

The Byerley Turk, first of the three foundation sires of the Thoroughbred to come to England. Painting by J. Wootton.

In 1689 Captain Byerley went with his regiment to Ireland to join the forces of William of Orange, taking the Byerley Turk as his charger. On one occasion he was nearly surrounded by a troop of King James II's cavalry but the speed of his stallion carried him to safety. The Byerley Turk was obviously much admired in Ireland as it is said offers of up to 3,000 guineas, a vast sum in those days, were refused for him. Instead Captain Byerley brought him back to his home Goldsborough Hall where the horse stood at stud.

According to Pick's Turf Register he did not cover many mares. His best racing offspring were Sprite, Black Hearty and Basto but his line was carried down through one son, Jigg, whose dam was a daughter of Spanker, by the D'Arcy Yellow Turk out of an untraceable mare. Jigg's son, Partner, out of a mare who was full sister of the Mixbury Galloway, became one of the best racehorses of the day and was said to be the finest stallion in the land. His son Tartar, out of Miliora by Fox, sired the great Herod foaled in 1758 from Cypron, by Blaze. It is through three of Herod's sons, Florizel, Woodpecker and Highflyer, that the Byerley Turk's line descends. In addition families founded by the Byerley Turk's daughters have also had a great influence in the Thoroughbred.

The Darley Arabian

Lady Wentworth, in her book *Thoroughbred Racing Stock*, quotes an extract from Thomas Darley's letter to Richard Darley, written at Aleppo on 21 December 1703:

> Since your father expects I should send him a stallion I esteem myself happy in a colt I bought a year and a half ago, with that design indeed per first opportunity; he comes four the latter end of March or the beginning of April next; his colour bay; and his near foot before with both his hind feet, have white upon them; he has a blaze down his face something of the largest; he is about 15 hands high; of the most esteemed race amongst the Arabs both by sire and dam, and the name of the race is called Manicha.

It would appear that portraits purported to be of the Darley Arabian and painted after his death could have been the cause of the insinuations made over 100 years later that he was not an Arabian. A similar assertion about the Godolphin Arabian is also connected with paintings, and since portraits of the famous horses of that

The Darley Arabian. Painting by J. Sartorius Senior.

period were often copied by other painters, or pupils, assumptions based on looks would seem to be of no dependable consequence.

Horses of the Darley Arabian male line through his son Flying Childers and the great Eclipse have an outstanding record in the Derby, both as winners and as sires of dams of winners.

The Godolphin Arabian

Most of the myths that surround the Godolphin Arabian were caused by arguments over the various prints purporting to be of this famous stallion, and began over 100 years after his importation from France.

The Godolphin Arabian, signed J. Wootton and dated 1731. Said by Lady Wentworth to be the best picture of the horse.

The Godolphin Arabian, or Sham as he was known, was one of four Arabians presented by the Bey of Tunis to the King of France in 1730. Mordaunt Milner, in his book *The Godolphin Arabian*, quoted the Vicomte de Manty who saw the Godolphin in France and gave the following description:

> He was of beautiful conformation, exquisitely proportioned with large hocks, well let down, with legs of iron, with unequalled lightness of forehand – a horse of incomparable beauty whose only flaw was being headstrong. An essentially strong stallion type, his quarters broad in spite of being half starved, tail carried in true Arabian style.

The vicomte is also quoted as describing the four horses as being in poor condition and thin when they were put in the Royal Stables, and disliked by the grooms as they were fiery and hard to ride. 'One of these was Shami, a bay brown with reddish mottle and very little white on his hind feet.' One of the myths concerning the Godolphin Arabian is that he was found pulling a water cart in France. Mr Milner dismisses this as nonsense but allows that every legend has a beginning, though becomes distorted in the re-telling.

The facts are that in 1730 Sham was sold to Edward Coke of Derbyshire. Mr Coke died in 1733; his mares were bequeathed to the Earl of Godolphin, who then bought Sham from Roger Williams, who had inherited Mr Coke's stallions. Thus Sham became known as the Godolphin Arabian.

Claims that the Godolphin Arabian was a Barb were largely made by writers who had seen various paintings purporting to be the Godolphin Arabian. It was also said that he was not as prepotent as the Byerley Turk and the Darley Arabian; but he was apparently sparingly used at stud and the veterinary surgeon, Osmer, is quoted as having written after Sham's death: 'It was a pity he was not used more universally for better mares.'

At stud the Godolphin Arabian proved to be an immediate success, several of his progeny being brilliant racehorses. It was, however, his son Cade, out of 'the lovely' Roxana, by Bald Galloway, who sired Matchem, whose name is given to the male line of the Godolphin Arabian, as was Eclipse to that of the Darley Arabian and Herod to that of the Byerley Turk.

Since the early descendants of these three great horses were often closely in-bred the amount of Arabian blood in the Thoroughbred was considerable through them alone. Add to this the many other Arabians stallions such as the Leedes Arabian, the Alcock Arabian and the Oxford Bloody Shouldered Arabian – and numerous oriental mares, and it can then be seen that the Thoroughbred breed owes its existence to the Arabians imported into England during the late seventeenth and eighteenth centuries.

Influence on light horse and pony breeding

It has been mentioned in previous chapters that most of the earliest horses exported from Arabia to countries around the world were used to upgrade local stock. In some instances new breeds were formed with horses carrying a high proportion of Arab blood in their veins; in many other cases Arabians were introduced to impart their special qualities with the result that there is hardly a breed of light horse that does not contain a percentage of Arab blood, and this applies to pony breeds as well. The Arabian is so prepotent that often the influence of one cross can be seen clearly several generations later.

The Barb

The Barb was a North African breed named after the region of its original home, Barbary, an area now consisting of Libya, Algeria and Morocco. Undoubtedly an ancient breed, it is in many respects similar to the Arabian from which it may have been derived, although experts differ on this. Barbs of palomino colouring, sometimes styled 'Golden horses', were taken by the Moors to Spain, and the Spanish in turn took them to Mexico.

The main differences between the Barb and the Arabian can be seen in the head and the hindquarters. The Barb has a larger ram-like head with a thicker muzzle and lacks the refinement and chiselled bone structure of the Arabian. The quarters are more sloping, and the tail set lower. The Barb can be rather wide between the hind legs; the mane and tail are thicker, and in general appearance it is coarser than the Arabian. Comparatively recently the two breeds have been crossed and the best Barbs, according to Lady Wentworth, are those with at least 50% Arab blood in their veins.

The Shagya

In 1839 Prince Pückler-Muskau visited the Babolna Stud in Hungary and particularly admired a powerfully built grey Arabian stallion of perfect symmetry which had been one of the group purchased in Syria by Major Freiherr von Herbert a few years earlier. He was called Shagya and was to become the foundation sire of one of the best families of the Arabian race in Europe, eventually to be known as a distinct breed named after their progenitor.

Shagya's progeny soon became greatly sought after, not only for their good looks, but also for their toughness and endurance under saddle and in harness; they were especially popular as cavalry horses. Shagya's sons and grandsons were from mares which were not all strictly purebred but carried much Arab blood. The stud books at Babolna were kept with great accuracy, and Shagyas were recorded from a very early time as a distinct group. They were interbred with careful selection and so developed into a very fine type of horse showing strong Arab characteristics. They make excellent all-round performance horses and are

Shagya stallion Grande Arab (1980), bred and owned by H. Nagel of Germany. He is of Babolna breeding being by Galan II ex Aysha by Amor.

very popular in many countries in Europe, principally Germany, Switzerland and Denmark.

The best known Shagya in England was Henry Wynmalen's Basa, registered as Shagya-XIII-3 (in the Hungarian system foals are given numbers after the name of their sire) and foaled at Count Esterhazy's stud in Hungary in 1930. Basa was brought to England by an army officer who had to re-sell the stallion when he was posted abroad. Basa was purchased by Mr Wynmalen and, in addition to making his name as a sire, was trained by his owner to Grand Prix standard in dressage. At that time dressage was practically unknown in Britain but Mr Wynmalen gave lectures and displays with Basa which became increasingly popular. To watch the proud, beautiful little grey stallion, superbly ridden by his owner, giving a display at the Royal Windsor Horse Show was an unforgettable experience, and such events were undoubtedly instrumental in the introduction and promotion of dressage in Britain.

Today most Shagyas are of over 90% Arab blood and the long selective breeding has ensured a genetic prepotency consistently producing beautiful carriage, balance, soundness, exceptional paces, intelligence and docility.

In addition to the Babolna Shagya Stud Book, Germany, Switzerland and Denmark have stud books of their own which come under a central international breed society, the Internationale Shagya-Gesellschaft (ISG). Several Eastern European countries with state studs are breeding Shagyas. Yugoslavia, Romania, Bulgaria and Czechoslovakia all have stud books of their own, but do not as yet come under the ISG. There is also considerable interest in the breed in the USA.

New management at Babolna has resulted in changes in policy and the stud is to concentrate more on Shagyas and reduce the number of Arabians. Egyptian blood had been introduced into the Shagyas and the horses were becoming smaller, so it has now been decided to import Shagyas from western Europe to Babolna.

Lipizzaner

One of the best-known breeds in Europe is the Lipizzaner, still being bred at one of the oldest studs in the world, Lipica, which was founded in 1580 by the Austrian Archduke Charles but is now in Yugoslavia.

The first horses to breed at Lipica came from Spain; they were famous for their proud and noble bearing and from them came the high-stepping 'Spanish Walk'. The vogue for high-school horses in the courts of Europe led to the establishment of the world-famous Spanish Riding School in Vienna and it is here that the Lipizzaners give their displays today.

In 1735 the recording of horses at Lipica led to the establishment of the Lipizzaner breed. Over the years stallions from other parts of Europe were bought for the stud, mainly from Spain, Italy, Germany and Denmark. Not all left lines in the stud and today all Lipizzaners trace in the male line to just six stallions, amongst them the Arabian Siglavy, who was foaled in 1810. Of the 19 female families recorded five were founded with Arabian mares.

Four Lipizzaner stallions from the Spanish Riding School in Vienna giving a high-school display.

Lipizzaners are nearly all grey, but can also be bay. They are about 15 h.h. to 16 h.h., strongly made and intelligent. In addition to giving their world-famous high-school displays in Vienna and on tour elsewhere, Lipizzaners are excellent harness horses and are selectively bred for performance ability.

The Orlov Trotter

Several old European breeds, notably the Orlov Trotter, owe their existence to

Arab and Barb horses. The Orlov Trotter was bred for harness racing and was developed by Count Orlov who in 1771 imported foundation stock, the first and most important of which was Smetanka, variously described as Arabian or Barb. A Danish mare of Spanish origin put to Smetanka produced Polkan and it was his son, Barss I (or Bars First), foaled in 1784 out of a Dutch mare, which was the progenitor of the breed. A tall handsome horse, the Orlov still shows the Arab influence. It became the world's supreme trotter, until ousted by the American Standardbred following the disruption of horse breeding during the Russian Revolution in 1917.

Other East European breeds founded with Arabian blood include the Karabair and the Malapolski.

The Tersk

A new breed created after the Russian Revolution is the Tersk, named after the stud in the North Caucasus. The Tersk Stud collected the few remaining horses of the Strelets breed, a large Arab-type breed based on native Ukrainian mares and Oriental sires, and crossed them with Arabians, Arab-Don cross-breds and Shagyas from Hungary. The Tersk breed was evolved at the Tersk and Stavropol Stud with the aim of producing a horse with the elegance, movement and endurance of the Arabian combined with the extreme toughness of native breeds of the area.

Warmbloods

All Warmbloods have similar backgrounds, and several European breeds such as the Hanoverian and the Cleveland Bay were founded by Arab blood upgrading local stock. In this group the Trakehner shows considerable Arabian influence, and some Warmbloods continue to allow Arab crosses.

The Gidran breed, however, took its name from the original Arabian stallion, Gidran Senior, imported into Hungary in 1816. Crossed with local mares and then Thoroughbreds, it later received further infusions of Arab blood. A stocky horse, it has been styled the Hungarian Anglo-Arab.

The Camargue

In western Europe the Camargue runs wild in the Rhone Delta in the south of

France, and is said to be descended from a very old breed, with some Arabian and half-bred stallions being introduced in the middle of the eighteenth century. Although small the Camargue is regarded as a horse rather than pony.

The Hispano/Arabe

Opinions differ on the origin of the Andalusian but some say it has much Arab influence. A new Spanish breed, the Hispano/Arabe, is the result of crossing the Andalusian with the Arabian. A new stud book for the breed was opened by the Jafatura de Lia Caballar in 1986 in Spain. The Cria Caballar have strict rules for the acceptance of stock for the foundation stud book, only animals of 50% Andalusian and 50% Arabian blood being admitted, with blood-typing of both parents.

American breeds

The influence of Arabians on light horse breeding has not been confined to Europe alone. In the USA the Morgan, a versatile breed with profuse tail-hair, dating from the 1780s, was founded by one stallion believed to have some Arab ancestry. The early Quarter Horse was heavily descended from Janus, a grandson of the Godolphin Arabian, and the modern day Appaloosa allows outside crosses to Thoroughbreds, Arabians and Quarter Horses only.

The Australian Stock Horse

The well-known Australian Waler was evolved from horses of Arabian, Barb, Dutch and Spanish ancestry, with more Arab, and Thoroughbred, blood added later. Once famous as a cavalry horse it has now found its place, as implied by its current name.

Pony breeds

Of the British pony breeds the New Forest, Dartmoor and Welsh have all had intermittent infusions of Arab blood – the Welsh Mountain pony in particular with its good proportions, elegance and lovely little head shows much Arab quality. The Scottish Highland pony has also been influenced by the introduction of Arab blood, as has the Irish Connemara.

Champion Welsh pony Dyoll Starlight.

On the Continent the well-known Haflinger breed in Austria is said to have been founded with Arab horses crossed with mountain ponies. The first written evidence of the breed in 1868 mentions an Arabian stallion from Babolna being used to upgrade the ponies; one of his sons, Folie, a chestnut with white mane and tail, became a foundation sire. In-breeding to Folie appears to have fixed the colour and type of these popular ponies.

Arabians have been used in Poland and the USSR to improve pony breeds, notably the Hucul in the Carpathian mountains and the Lokai in Uzbekistan. As with breeds of horses in Eastern Europe, much of the foundation stock contained Arabian blood, since over the centuries importations from Arabia were constantly arriving to be used for up-grading.

A French breed, the Landais, also has ancient origins and has been greatly influenced by Arab blood over the years. Even as late as 1913 an Arabian stallion was introduced and the Landais ponies, which are quite small, around 13 h.h., have many Arab features.

The South African Basuto pony has been up-graded with Arab blood since the seventeenth century and it too shows Arab qualities.

Anglo-Arabs

The make-up of the Anglo-Arab can vary slightly in different countries. Basically it is the result of crossing Arabians and Thoroughbreds but in some countries the foundation stock has included on the Thoroughbred side horses of slightly mixed breeding, which could also be said of the original animals that founded the Thoroughbred in England.

The British Anglo-Arab Stud Book is confined to horses having only pure Arabian and registered Thoroughbred ancestors. The first volume of the Stud Book was published in 1938, and by 1990 ten volumes had been published. Between 1985 and 1990 an average of 125 animals were registered each year.

It is interesting that despite the closure of the Arabian section in Weatherby's General Stud Book (GSB) in 1965, there are today a number of British-bred Anglo-Arabs which are GSB registered. Many people consider a certain degeneracy is showing in present-day Thoroughbred racehorses and if breeders decided that a fresh infusion of Arabian blood would be beneficial these Anglo-Arabs in the GSB could be of great significance.

The Anglo-Arab, with its size and scope, is more popular than the Arabian for performance work with those who prefer a larger horse, and they have been successful in many spheres in Britain. The British Olympic dressage horse, Prince Consort, is an Anglo of 25% Arabian blood and there are numerous others competing with success in dressage, eventing and other disciplines.

Anglo-Arabs can be first crosses of Thoroughbred mares with Arabian stallions or vice versa, or they can be produced by breeding Thoroughbred to Anglo or

Champion Anglo-Arab of 50% Arab blood, Dancing Instructor (1964). He was one of a very successful family bred by Mr and Mrs K. A. Smith from their Thoroughbred mare Dark Continent by the purebred Manto. Dancing Instructor dominated the Anglo-Arab section of the AHS Show for six years when he was Male Champion from 1968 to 1973.

Arabian to Anglo, or Anglo to Anglo: thus the amount of Arabian blood in Anglo-Arabs varies enormously and leads to individuals of different appearance. Breeding Anglo to Anglo, especially if both horses are similar in size and looks, is far more likely to establish a distinct breed and this is what the French have done.

The origin of the breed in France goes back to 1820 when three imported Thoroughbred mares, Deer, Comus Mare and Selim Mare, were put to two stallions at the Royal Stud of Le Pin: Aslan, of Turkish origin, and the famous Massoud, an Arabian, who was considered the real foundation sire of the breed. Their progeny were put to the best imported Thoroughbred stallions, and produced many brilliant racehorses.

Twenty-three years later, when the management of the Royal Stud had been taken over by Eugene Gayot, most of the daughters and granddaughters of the three foundation mares were moved to Pompadour, previously known for its stud of Arabians under Louis XV's mistress, Madame de Pompadour. It was found that the mares produced their best stock when put to Arabians; as described by Eugene Gayot the Anglo-Arab 'has longer lines, more size, is stronger and has more substance than the Arab; better in his ribs, he shows less daylight, is more compact than the Thoroughbred horse, less high strung in temper and his produce less nervous'.

The Anglo-Arab was then carefully developed by selective breeding and in the early days was bred mainly for military use. Since 1930 the French have been using Anglo-Arab stallions extensively and after the Second World War the breed was developed for its exceptional versatility as a riding horse.

Today the Anglo-Arab is one of the most highly prized breeds in the country and many leading French riders in show jumping and eventing have been mounted on Anglos. In France the Anglo-Arab must carry a minimum of 25% Arab blood and the stallions are used in producing the Selle Française, the modern breed of French competition horse.

Partbred Arabs

Horses or ponies which are cross-bred with Arabians are classified as partbred Arabs in Britain, while in some countries they are known as Arab-bred or Arab race. In Britain, to be eligible for registration in the British Arab Horse Society Partbred Register, animals have to have a minimum of 25% Arabian blood. They can be bred from almost any other breed or mixture of breeds, which results in partbreds ranging from small children's ponies to large riding horses, or even heavier types of horse for harness work.

In keeping with its stated aim to encourage the re-introduction of Arab blood into English light horse breeding the AHS produced its first Arab-bred Register in 1921. There are now 14 Partbred Arab Registers and a yearly average of 550 animals were registered between 1985 and 1990.

One of the most famous partbred Arab families originated in Ireland. In 1937 Mrs Stephanie Nicholson purchased a purebred colt, Naseel (Raftan ex Naxina), from the Hanstead Stud and took him to her home in County Meath with the idea of producing from local mares better ponies for performance, temperament and beauty. Naseel was an unqualified success and his record as a sire of children's ponies must be unique; in addition his progeny included champion hacks and even heavyweight cobs.

The most famous family of all were the progeny of Naseel and Gipsy Gold, a 13 h.h. chestnut mare with Welsh Pony and Thoroughbred blood in her pedigree but described as a true pony in appearance. Gipsy Gold produced a string of champion show ponies by Naseel. The best known, Pretty Polly, foaled in 1945, was unbeaten in six years of showing. She, with her sister My Pretty Maid, and brother, the

Pretty Polly (1945) by Naseel ex Gipsy Gold, matriarch of one of the most famous families of children's ponies, at the AHS Show, Roehampton, in 1956. Naseel and some of his champion progeny were invited to parade before HM The Queen who was visiting the show that year.

Mrs S. Nicholson's Naseel, one of the most famous sires of children's ponies. Bred by Lady Yule at Hanstead he was by Skowronek's grandson Raftan (Naseem ex Riyala) out of a Skowronek daughter, Naxina, and stood only 14.1 h.h.

gelding Eureka, broke all known records when they were champion, reserve and runner-up at the Royal International and at the Horse of the Year Show in 1951.

Pretty Polly was not only a champion children's pony, she proved to be equally successful as a brood mare. Some of her progeny and their offspring were exported and achieved fame in the USA and in Australia. In England her sons and daughters have had a colossal influence on pony breeding with numerous champions

Partbred Arab, Pipers Green Blue Haze (1978) by Pipers Green King of the Desert out of Pipers Green Golden Domino, bred by Mrs J. Rust. A consistent winner, she was the Over 14.2 h.h. Champion, AHS Show, 1987.

descended from them and this influence can still be seen in many of the outstanding ponies of today.

The success of the partbred Arabs is not just confined to ponies in the show ring; many horses have reached the top in performance events. Amongst others, the well-known show jumper, Rex the Robber, was by the Arabian Noran; and Spinning Rhombus, the second highest placed horse in the New Zealand team which won the Gold Medal in the 1990 Three Day Event at the International Equestrian Games in Stockholm, was bred in England out of a half-Arabian mare. Some of the world's best long distance horses are partbred Arabs, including Wyere Lad, who has won many events, General Portfolio Hero (Arab/Thoroughbred/Irish Draught cross) and Alfie (Arab/cob cross), both of which helped the British team to win the Gold Medal for endurance at Stockholm in 1990.

7 The Arab Horse Society

The Arab Horse Society was founded on 24 March 1918. It is recorded that it was the Rev. D. B. Montefiore 'to whose initiative the chief credit for promoting the foundation of the Society must be given'. The Rev. Montefiore, who was a breeder of polo ponies and a past president of the National Pony Society, was convinced that it would be in the breed's interest to have its own society and stud books.

He was not alone in those views, for Mr Musgrave Clark recalled lunching with the Rev. Montefiore on several occasions in Brighton during the First World War and finding that they shared the same ideal of a society to represent the breed in England.

The Rev. Montefiore sent letters to 24 people whose interest in Arabians was known to him and early in March 1918 met Mr S. G. Hough and Mr Clark in Newmarket. Both were enthusiastic. He then sent invitations to a meeting at the Grosvenor Hotel in London.

The Rev. Montefiore took the chair at the meeting and it was proposed by Sydney Hough and seconded by Mr W. A. Willis that the society be formed and called 'The Arab Horse Society'. Others present were Mr H. V. M. Clark and Mr S. Cochrane, and the proposal was carried unanimously. Nineteen letters of warm approval were read out and the first council meeting of the Society was then held.

Mr Willis was voted to the Chair and the Rev. Montefiore was appointed Secretary. Mr Clark proposed that Wilfrid Blunt be nominated as the first President, Mr Blunt having intimated he would accept, and this was seconded by Mr Cochrane and passed unanimously. The annual membership subscription was fixed at one guinea and entry fees for the stud book were to be ten shillings for stallions and mares.

During the early formative years the Society was run by a dedicated few who continued in the belief that it had come into being not for breeders, nor for owners, but for the good of the breed itself. This belief has been paramount in the minds of the many people who, over more than 70 years, have worked hard in the interests of the Arab horse. The AHS could not have achieved half of what it has been able to do and continues to do, were it not for the army of voluntary helpers, of all ages, who assist with the running of the many events organised by, or under the umbrella of, the Society.

On 4 March 1919 the newly formed Society staged a class for Arab stallions at a show in Newmarket. It was won by Dolmatscher, a grey stallion bred in Germany at the Weil Stud and owned by Duncan MacDougall; Nureddin II in the ownership of Mr S. G. Hough was second and Skowronek, at that time still owned by Mr H. V. M. Clark, came third.

The following year the AHS joined the National Pony Society at their show, which was held each spring at the Agricultural Hall, Islington; there were classes for purebred stallions, mares and youngstock and a riding class; they also had a section for Arab-bred horses. This became an annual event, known as the London Show, and continued with gradually increasing entries and classes up to the outbreak of the Second World War. The Society was also active in encouraging classes for Arabians at major shows in the country and one or two were held even during the war.

The first performance event to be held by the AHS was an endurance ride of 300 miles to test stamina. It took place at Lewes in Sussex, in October 1920, and was ridden over five consecutive days with careful vetting throughout. This memorable first event was won by Mr L. Edmund's Shahzada, with Robin belonging to Mr C. W. Hough and Belka and Mustapha Kemel in the ownership of Mr H. V. M. Clark winning silver medals. Two more similar rides were held in 1921, when Belka won, and in 1922 when Shahzada was again the winner.

These rides were discontinued, but in 1923 a race of one mile was run at Bideford under National Pony Turf Club rules, which was won by Belka. In 1928 a race open to Arabians in the AHS Stud Book was run over 1¼ miles at the Portsmouth Races, when Mr H. V. M. Clark's stallions Ferdaan and Sainfoin were first and second respectively, with the Pony Turf Club guaranteeing the stakes. The following year two races were run at Northolt Park over distances of 1¼ and 1½ miles, with the same two horses coming first and second, but in reverse name order.

In those days the AHS had to rely on the existing racing authorities to provide races at their meetings and due to their reluctance to do so no more Arab racing took place between the two world wars.

During this time the number of breeders gradually grew and the Society began producing registers for Arab-bred stock, in addition to the stud book for purebreds. The demand was mainly for horses to be used for hacking and the aim was to encourage the reintroduction of Arabian blood into light horse and pony breeding.

The governing body of the Society is the Council. In 1922 it was agreed that elections to Council would be for a period of three years, with one third of the members retiring each year. This system is still in operation and there is now a

One of the early shows at the Royal Agricultural Hall, Islington.

Council of 30. The President is elected annually by Council, and the immediate Past-President and the President-Elect are in close touch with the current President, which helps to ensure continuity.

Initially the Secretary carried out all the office work, including the registration of horses. By 1922 200 people had joined the Society and by the Second World War there were just over 300 members. Brigadier W. H. Anderson, who succeeded the Rev. Montefiore as Secretary, worked from an office in his home up to 1951 when he retired through ill health. Colonel R. C. de V. Askin took over as Secretary and for the next 16 years he also ran the Society from his home but with secretarial help. During his tenure the membership rose to 1,000. More studs were being founded and since the Secretary also acted as Treasurer and show director the work grew substantially.

The 'boom' years came in the 1960s and early 1970s and by 1973 the membership had topped the 3,000 mark. Since then there have been fluctuations and with double membership now allowed (under which any two people may belong on one double subscription) the actual number of subscribers in 1990 is still around 3,000.

A rapid rise in the number of studs formed and horses bred meant the job had become too large for one person and in 1969 a Registration Department was opened in Cranbrook at the home of the late Colin Pearson, who was made the Society's first Registrar. Thirteen years later the office of the Secretary was moved to Cranbrook so that all the activities could more conveniently be run from one centre, and Mr Pearson became Chief Administrator; he worked devotedly for the breed and the Society until his sudden death five years later.

The 1980s saw a tremendous increase in the Society's work. In addition to running annual shows and several performance events, Arab racing had begun again and was becoming one of the major activities of the Society. The first meeting was held at Hawthorn Hill on 10 July 1978, and it attracted 31 runners. From this small beginning Arab racing grew steadily. It is run by the AHS under the jurisdiction of the Jockey Club (the governing body of Thoroughbred racing) and as a result meetings are allowed on licensed racecourses throughout the country.

In addition to the increasing number of foal registrations and transfers of ownership, the Registration Department also had to deal with increasing imports; work in all departments escalated and the office staff grew.

After Colin Pearson's death in 1987 the Society had to seek new offices. The possibility of purchasing permanent premises, rather than continuing to rent, had already been considered and the following year Windsor House, a property in the

Wiltshire village of Ramsbury, was purchased. In 1989 the Society moved in and now operates from its own building.

The activities organised by the AHS are many and varied. Committees, made up of elected Council members, with the power to co-opt others, run the various events; these committee categories are: Show and Judges' Selection; Racing; Stud Book and Registration; General Purposes and Education; and Ridden Events. Each committee elects its own chairman and reports back to the Council. The Council usually meets about four times a year. Newsletters go round to members four times a year giving general information and the AGM is held each spring. All the office work is done from the Society's headquarters and currently there are ten permanent staff at Windsor House. However, as already pointed out, a large number of people work voluntarily to assist with the practicalities of running the events.

The annual shows

One of the most important events in the Society's calendar is the annual Summer Show, which runs for three days and is generally held in the last week of July. Not only is it a pleasant gathering where old friends meet   for visitors come from many overseas countries as well as from all over Britain – but the show is also the shop window of the breed.

The largest breed show in Europe, it caters for Anglo-Arabs and partbreds (divided into two sections – over 14.2 h.h. and under 14.2 h.h.) in addition to purebreds. There are ridden classes for all sections, including one for junior riders, side-saddle and pairs; recent innovations have been a class for racehorses and one for young handlers. The sire produce class and family groups through the female line are of particular interest and use to breeders. There are also futurity classes for youngstock.

Traditionally held at a London venue, the Society's first annual Summer Show took place in the attractive setting of Roehampton polo ground in 1946. The ending of polo at Roehampton and the extension of the golf course necessitated a different venue, so in 1958 the show was held at Richmond and subsequently at Kempton Park until 1975, when departure from the proximity of London was tried. The venue, Peterborough, was not popular and in 1977 the show returned south, to be held at Ascot Paddocks. However, as the show's size increased so it became increasingly obvious that the limited area available at Ascot could no longer accommodate it, for mounted competitors lacked the necessary space for exercise before classes. A reluctant decision had to be taken to move and as London sites proved impracticable the show went in 1990 to the Three Counties showground at Malvern Wells.

Entries totalled between 1,000 and 1,200 from 1985 to 1990, with such large numbers of purebred yearlings and two-year-olds entered that these classes have had to be separated into anything up to four divisions. In recent years entries in the ridden classes have also increased dramatically.

In 1975 a show was organised in the north of England at Haydock Park racecourse. Called the Northern AHS Show, it has become an annual two-day event, usually held in the second half of June. This show also caters for Anglos and partbreds as well as purebreds, and classes are similar to those of the main show, but without produce classes, though including those for costume and driving. The title of British National Champion is awarded only at the main Summer Show.

Racing

There were two Arab race meetings in 1978 and the number grew steadily up to 1985 when the first International meeting was held at Kempton Park, sponsored by the Emirate of Dubai. H. H. Sheikh Hamdan bin Rashid Al Maktoum has been a most generous supporter of Arab racing in Britain. After 1986 the number of meetings grew rapidly until in 1990 there were 21.

Arab racing is an amateur sport in that no professional trainers or jockeys are allowed an AHS licence to train or ride; the actual organisation is run very professionally and strict rules, approved by the Jockey Club, are adhered to.

In 1990, 426 owners, 226 trainers, 248 jockeys and 516 horses were registered with the Society for racing purposes. Horses are divided into three grades according to their racing record, with a weight allowance and some special races for mares. Usually each meeting has two races for Anglo-Arabs and it is hoped to reintroduce racing for partbreds. This had to be curtailed by direction of the Jockey Club until blood-typing rules for the acceptance of racehorses similar to those in operation for the registration of Anglos could be implemented.

Championship races for sprints and long distance are held each year, as well as a mare championship, but the highlights of the season are the International meetings. In addition to the annual Kempton Park International Day, a second meeting was held in 1990 at Windsor, sponsored by the President of the United Arab Emirates,

Arab Sheikhs watching a class of brood mares and foals at the 1989 AHS Show at Kempton Park.

Sheikh Zayed Bin Sultan Al Nahyan. The two open races at each meeting have attracted runners from several European countries, with horses from France tending to dominate the scene.

The magazine

'The Council of our Society has for some time past given serious thought to the desirability of issuing from time to time a publication concerning the Arab horse in general and the activities of the Society in particular.' These were the words of Brigadier Anderson in the preface to the first magazine produced by the AHS in 1935. It was decided it should take the form of an annual journal concerning Arab horse matters, which would be of interest not only to members but to others. Four issues of *The Arab Horse* were published up to 1938 and then the outbreak of war prevented further publication.

It was not until 1955 that the Society resumed the publication of a magazine, but that year the first issue of *The Arab Horse Society News* heralded the introduction of an important part of the Society's work. Published twice a year, it has grown from a slim but well-produced 47-page magazine into a handsome publication of about 140 pages, which has recently been described as the 'best Arab horse magazine in Europe'. Certainly it has remained in existence far longer than any other, and with many colour photographs plus numerous stud advertisements, it acts as the main publicity organ for the Society's breeders.

In addition to reporting on the Society's annual shows, race meetings, dressage competitions, Marathon Race and other events, the magazine carries articles on a

Magic Knight (1978) by Sir Lancelot out of Magic Flare, bred by the Hawkhurst Stud. A true family racehorse, owned by Mrs Gina Webster, trained by her husband John and ridden by daughter Alison. In the 1980s he ran in 41 races, won 12, second in 9 and third in 9. In the International Six Furlong Race at Kempton Park, he was fourth and best British horse in 1985 and 1988, second in 1986 and third in 1987.

variety of subjects such as endurance riding and well-known horses and studs; the personalities and achievements of individual horses and their riders are also recorded. There is an international section containing news from overseas and a section for junior riders; veterinary articles, book reviews and letters to the editor feature regularly. The magazine is sent to all members of the AHS and is also sold through the Society and some British and overseas booksellers.

The Marathon and other events

The Marathon Race, run over the Olympic distance of 26¼ miles, is an annual event in the AHS calendar. It is open to horses of any breed but is usually dominated by those of Arab breeding. It was first held in 1974 and has had a number of venues around the country since then. A real test of endurance and courage, there is very strict veterinary supervision during the race with compulsory walking and trotting sections, and all horses finishing have to pass a final veterinary inspection.

The Ride and Tie, for two competitors and one horse with the riders alternatively running and riding, is another test of human and equine fitness. This event has been held most years since the 1970s and is also open to all breeds.

Each year the AHS awards several trophies for performance horses. These competitions are worked out on a points system and marks are given in a wide variety of disciplines, ranging from ridden show classes and dressage to hunter trials and eventing. There are three principal trophies for Arabians, Anglo-Arabs and partbreds respectively. A new competition started in 1990 is for the winning high-point Arabian in endurance riding, with marks given in recognised rides throughout the season. With championships for ridden Anglos and partbreds and AHS merit rosettes to be won at shows around the country which are affiliated to the Society, there is a range of awards for which members can compete.

The AHS has a judges' panel, divided into sections for international or national judges, for in-hand and for riding classes. Prospective judges are invited to the Society's selection courses and have to pass quite stiff tests and scrutiny before their names go before Council who vote on their election to the panel. Other courses held include stud management and riding clinics, and the Society distributes leaflets on many subjects connected with horse-keeping and riding. An innovation for 1991 is the introduction of a scholarship towards further training for horses and riders participating in competitions.

133

The 1984 AHS Marathon over Exmoor. Mrs J. Brimecombe and Tashkir (1977) by Magento ex Shimaal, bred by Mr and Mrs A. Dennis, on the moors above Stoke Pero. They finished fourth.

There are 18 Regional Groups throughout the country, the first to be established being the Scottish Group which was founded in 1965. Each group runs its own programme of events which include in-hand and performance shows, stud visits, talks and demonstrations and with social gatherings also held there are enjoyable opportunities for members to get together. There is also an annual inter-regional dressage competition, which was held in 1990 in conjunction with the Summer Show.

The registration department

The registration department is always busy. Foals are registered in their first year but before any Arabian or Anglo-Arab can be used for breeding it has to be blood-typed and entered as a mature breeding animal; stallions must pass a veterinary inspection and both sexes must be 24 months old before acceptance. All changes of ownership have to be recorded, and horses sold abroad need special papers dealing with their acceptance into the stud books of the country of their exportation. Those imported into England have their full details checked and approved by the Stud Book and Registration Committee before they are accepted into the Society's Stud Book. An average of 900 purebred foals are registered each year. In 1990 covering certificate books were issued to approximately 1,000 purebred stallions. The entire population of Arabians in the UK is estimated to be 15,000. Imports have risen dramatically in the last two years, with 114 registered in 1990, whilst exports numbered 90.

In addition to printing studbooks for purebreds and Anglo-Arabs and a register for partbreds, the Society produces a Stud Directory every two years. This booklet is compiled from returns sent in by stud owners and is a very useful guide to stud farms throughout the UK and the horses each stud possesses. The Arab Horse Stud Book records the produce of mares over every four year period, and in the years between publication a Return of Mares booklet is brought out.

8 The position of the breed in the 1990s

The earlier chapters of this book have shown how for centuries the Arabian was used all over the world to up-grade local horses and ponies and as a foundation stock for the creation of new breeds.

At around the turn of the century breeders everywhere were discovering that high-class Arab horses were becoming difficult to find in Arabia. It came to be generally recognised that it was essential to maintain breeding stocks of purebred Arabs in countries outside the Middle East. This in turn made possible the great increase in popularity of the Arabian in the second half of the twentieth century.

But paradoxically a boom in a breed creates its own problems. Over-enthusiastic production of whatever breed happens to be currently 'popular' can be detrimental to the general good of that breed. Fashions can change – and they can change a breed too.

Early breeders stressed the fact that the best of the authentic Arabians were near perfect. They warned that to try to 'improve' could be counter-productive, as breeding too specifically for any one quality could result in the loss of that exquisite harmony of parts which adds up to the sum of the whole so effectively in the finest specimens. This is not to assert that all Arabians are perfection itself, but that wise breeders were quick to cull from breeding stock any horse which did not meet high standards. Faults are bound to appear in any domestic breed and they are best eliminated gradually by selective breeding. Indiscriminate over-production, there-fore, presents dangers; but the temptation to produce more as quickly as possible proves irresistible to many breeders when prices are high. Eventually the market becomes flooded; prices begin to drop and opportunists who jumped on bandwagons during good times are the first to get off when a slump appears inevitable. This has happened throughout the history of horse breeding and yet it seems that breeders as a whole are slow to learn from past mistakes of others.

The biggest Arabian 'boom' came in the USA when horse breeding brought tax benefits. Many businessmen started up as 'breeders', though often they kept their animals at livery with trainers and hardly ever saw them. Keep charges were high and those who ran livery stables made a handsome profit. There was keen competition to own National Champion Arabians; indeed, the incentive to win became so great that all kinds of manipulations were practised. Some of these constituted equine abuse, but with owners spurring on the trainers to win at all costs matters became worse – and it was the horses that suffered. It seems ironic that the very beauty of the Arabian came to be the cause of one of its saddest problems. More people wanted to own these lovely horses but many only wished to see them as creatures to admire prancing round a show ring. Auction sales of theatrical proportions led to vastly inflated prices, many of which were rigged and bore no relation to the real value of the horse. This led to different 'grades' of Arabian, with the 'million dollar' show horse at the top, down through the sensibly priced high-quality horse to the sub-standard specimen resulting from over-breeding with inferior stock.

Over the last two decades this basic problem in the USA has had an effect on some other countries. Although the vast majority of American Arab horse owners are well aware of the problems in the Arabian horse industry, as it has become known, and deplore some of the showing practices (such as whip abuse, artificial aids and even cosmetic surgery to 'improve' the animal), this showing fashion spread to Canada and some European countries. A further problem arose with the training of these 'fashionable' show horses. They were made to stand stretched, with heads high in the air and the nose almost horizontal. In the beginning this pose was a disguise for poor conformation of back and hind quarters, neck, or legs but, like all new fashions, it soon became exaggerated. The 'Jersey cow look', as one senior and very experienced British judge once described it (with back practically level and nowhere to put the saddle), is not correct for an Arabian – but this is how some have been misled into thinking it should appear. In addition a horse trained by these methods to show in-hand finds it difficult to adjust to ordinary riding; also it can be temperamentally spoilt for life. In many cases the horses are kept so 'hyped up' that they are unable to relax and stand as nature intended, thus jeopardising true judging. A serious consideration is that showing in this manner makes the horse look different to the genuine classic Arabian – the ideal most properly to be aimed for.

When the 1970s US boom with its accompanying show-ring fashions for Arabians spread to Canada, there were some outspoken comments, particularly over the presentation of the horses in Park Horse classes. In these classes riders sit right back and the horses, with the 'aid' of weighted shoes and over-long feet, are trained to trot with unnaturally high and jerky knee action. Many breeders in Canada and the USA are now so disillusioned with modern showing practices that they are banding together to hold shows run on conventional lines, often with owners themselves exhibiting their animals.

Liquidambar (1984) by Indian Diadem out of Bright Reflexion, bred by the Duchess of Rutland and ridden by Mrs Caroline Nelson. With many wins under saddle, Liquidambar was the Best Mare at the AHS Show for three successive years (1989–91) and Overall Ridden Champion in 1989 and 1991.

Showing, however, is only one side of the competitive picture; happily there is a much healthier aspect. Interest in the ridden Arabian rapidly increased during the 1970s and 1980s. As outlined earlier, endurance riding is now a popular sport and provides an excellent chance for horses of Arabian breeding to prove their worth in the performance field. With purebreds as well as Anglo-Arabs and partbreds competing in dressage, show jumping and a whole range of ridden disciplines, more and more riders are becoming aware of the versatility of the breed. In Britain and the USA in particular racing has caught the imagination of many people and extended yet again the range of activities in which the Arab horse can excel.

Riding in nearly all Western countries is on the increase and the Arabian is gaining in popularity as an all-round riding animal. Many of the increased number of Arab horses throughout the world are leading a useful life under saddle, but breeders need to take great care to preserve the true qualities of the breed. There have been suggestions that two types of Arabian are being bred: one for in-hand showing and the other for performance. This is entirely unnecessary – in England a British National Champion colt has gone on to become a race winner. It is up to breeders, owners, judges and all those who admire the breed to ensure that the 'near perfect' authentic Arabian remains as nature intended it to be. Judges have an important role to play in this respect.

Another consequence of the rapid rise in the world's Arab horse population has been the emergence of many new stud books. In 1972 the World Arabian Horse Organisation (WAHO) came into being following a meeting in London of representatives from 13 countries. One of the organisation's principal activities has been to encourage Arab horse breeding countries to produce stud books to a required standard. This is to ensure the accurate and consistent registration of foals.

WAHO now has a list of acceptable stud books in countries throughout the world. The conditions which have to be met before they are accepted by WAHO have ensured that far better records are now being kept than ever before. Blood-typing is becoming a regular practice in many countries; all Arabians exported from Britain have to be blood-typed.

Some other European countries have had compulsory stallion licencing with horses having to pass a veterinary and performance test, as well as reaching a required standard in breed characteristics, quality and conformation. However, these regulatory tests have not been entirely satisfactory, and some countries are now doing away with them. There is no similar scheme in Britain, where stallions are licensed solely by veterinary inspection. Within the European Economic Community it seems likely that veterinary tests for stallions will be accepted by all Arab horse societies.

The most noticeable recent developments in the Arab horse scene in Britain are: the fashion of showing Arabians in-hand (mostly at international shows) in the style referred to above (although this has not affected Anglo-Arabs and partbreds); the evolvement of Arab racing; and a staggering increase in the number of imports.

The new fashion in showing has come in from the Continent, although it has come to be described as 'American'. It is true that the 'head in the air' stance originated in the USA but whip abuse has been known in at least one country on the Continent for some time.

It must be said that the more serious forms of abuse are only carried out by a very small minority of trainers and handlers, but such matters as gingering (applying ginger to make the horse raise its tail) and the shaving of parts of the head are more widely practised. In the view of the vast majority of exhibitors most of these practices, originally designed to alter or 'improve' the natural image of the horse, are considered to be a form of deception.

Many of the horses subjected to these showing methods are really good specimens, and would win on merit without any artificial 'aids', but inexperienced or new exhibitors, on seeing horses shown in this manner winning, mistakenly believe that they must do likewise if they are to compete with success, thus compounding a serious problem.

The British Arab Horse Society has made new rules and regulations and is taking strong action to enforce them with disciplinary committees appointed at their main shows. In 1984 the European Conference of Arab Horse Organisations (ECAHO) was formed and its Show Committee made strict rules applicable at all affiliated shows. By 1991 most international shows, national shows and the major regional shows are so affiliated.

It is vital to ensure that rules are strictly enforced if undesirable and often cruel abuses are to be stamped out. Europe could learn from the experience of exhibitors in the USA where rules have not always been applied firmly; many people have given up showing their Arabians in-hand as a protest against practices abhorred by the vast majority.

The rapid development of racing in Britain has given many new enthusiasts of the breed an enjoyable pursuit. In addition to providing a purposeful existence for many geldings it provides an incidental test of breeding stock's soundness and temperament, as happens in the USSR and Poland. However, it is important to ensure that the breed's true characteristics are never sacrificed in the interests of breeding for speed alone.

The enormous increase in the number of horses imported into Britain in the last two years - in 1990 the number of imports was one-third of the total brought in

A blanket finish to the Wilsford Stakes at Larkhill in 1990. Silvena (4) just beat Rezah's Tiger Lily (1) by a short head. Pharissa (7) finished fourth.

during the years 1969 to 1988 – is the most recent development. Part of this increase can be attributed to a considerable number of Russian-bred horses brought in for racing. In 1990 some of them proved excellent racehorses, but their value as breeding stock will take a decade or two to be truly assessed. WAHO's work with stud books has no doubt helped to encourage the movement of horses from one country to another.

The success of Arabians and their derivatives in endurance riding has already been described. The fact that they are also becoming more prominent in dressage and other disciplines is encouraging for the breed's future.

British-bred Arabians exported to various countries are proving their worth in showing and performance spheres, as well as for breeding, and in the show rings of Europe British horses are winning their fair share of awards.

Many of the successful horses which help promote the breed come from small studs or belong to one-horse owners; their contribution should never be underestimated or eclipsed by the larger studs which naturally attract greater publicity and whose owners can better afford to keep their horses in the public eye.

Provided breeders are careful, do not allow themselves to become overstocked and appreciate that the Arabian's special attributes of beauty, endurance, soundness and temperament are qualities which must never be lost in their stock, the future for the breed in Britain should be assured.

On the Continent there has been a pattern of events similar to that in Britain – except that Arab racing has not developed as dramatically as it has in England. The show rings, on the whole, have been dominated by a comparatively few owners. Whether this is for the good of the breed in the long term is debatable – it tends to set 'fashions' and certain horses could dominate the scene to the extent that 'popular' lines may become too in-bred, thereby risking degeneracy. The idea mentioned above of two 'kinds' of Arabian developing – one for riding and another for the show ring – is a matter which all breeders should be seriously considering; any such division cannot benefit the breed as a whole.

It is noticeable that ridden classes in Continental shows are far less popular than those in Britain, which are now well supported. Perhaps if special encouragement was given to the horses which are successful both in-hand and under saddle any such division could be more easily overcome.

In North America, Australia and South Africa there is far more emphasis on the ridden Arabian at shows than is the case in Europe.

A recent world gathering noted that there is a steady growth in the Arab horse population and that more emphasis is being placed on performance by many countries. The problems of over-production will not ease unless the old dictum 'quality rather than quantity' is followed by all breeders.

Bibliography

The Arabian Horse in Australia (Arabian Horse Society of Australia, 1990)

Archer, Fleming. *Lady Anne Blunt: Journals and Correspondence* (Alexander Heriot, 1986)

Archer, Rosemary, Pearson, Colin and Covey, Cecil. *The Crabbet Arabian Stud: Its History and Influence* (Alexander Heriot, 1978)

Blunt, Lady Anne. *A Pilgrimage to Nejd* (Murray, 1881)

Blunt, Lady Anne. *The Bedouin Tribes of the Euphrates* (Murray, 1879)

Blunt, Wilfrid Scawen. *My Diaries* (M. Secker, 1919)

Borden, Spencer. *The Arab Horse* (Doubleday, Page & Co., 1906; reprinted 1961)

Brown Edwards, Gladys. *The Arabian War Horse to Show Horse* (The Arabian Horse Trust of America, 1969)

Brown, W. R. *The Horse of the Desert* (Macmillan, 1947)

Flynn, Joan, and Gordon, Coralie. *The Crabbet Arabian Imports to Australia* (Somerset Publications, 1988)

Forbis, Judith. *The Classic Arabian Horse* (Liveright, 1976)

Gordon, Coralie. *The Crabbet Silver Family in Australia* (Somerset Publications, 1987)

Greely, Margaret. *Arabian Exodus* (J. A. Allen, 1975)

Haralambos, K. M. *The Byerley Turk* (Threshold, 1990)

Hyland, Ann. *The Endurance Horse* (J. A. Allen, 1988)

Jurkovic, Dr Joze. *Kobilarna Lipica* (Lipica, Yugoslavia, n.d. [1990])

Kidd, Jane. *An Illustrated International Encyclopedia of Horse Breeds and Breeding* (Salamander, c.1985)

Milner, Mordaunt. *The Godolphin Arabian* (J. A. Allen, 1990)

Mohamed Aly, H. H. Prince. *Breeding of Pure Bred Arab Horses* (c. 1976)

Parkinson, Mary Jane. *The Kellogg Arabian Ranch: The First Sixty Years* (Cal Poly Kellogg Unit Foundation, 1975)

Pearson, Colin, with Mol, Kees. *The Arabian Horse Families of Egypt from 1870 to 1980* (Alexander Heriot, 1988)

Raswan, Carl. *The Arab and His Horse* (Oakland, Calif., 1955)

Schiele, Erika. *The Arab Horse in Europe* (Harrap, 1970)

Sherbatov, Prince A. G., and Stroganov, Count S. A. *The Arabian Horse* (J. A. Allen, 1989)

Struben, Pamela. *Horses and Riding in Southern Africa* (Purnell, 1966)

Summerhays, R. S. *The Arabian Horse* (Wilshire Book Company, 1969)

Tweedie, Major-General W. *The Arabian Horse: His Country and People* (Blackwood, 1894)

Upton, Peter. *The Arab Horse* (Crowood, 1989)

Upton, Roger D. *Newmarket and Arabia: An Examination of the Descent of Racers and Coursers* (Henry S. King, 1873)

Vesey-Fitzgerald, Brian. *The Book of the Horse* (Nicholson & Watson, 1946)

Wentworth, Lady. *The Authentic Arabian Horse and His Descendants* (Allen & Unwin, 1945)

Wentworth, Lady. *Thoroughbred Racing Stock and Its Ancestors* (Allen & Unwin, 1938)

Wentworth, Lady. *The World's Best Horse* (Allen & Unwin, 1958)

Wentworth, Lady. *The Swift Runner* (Allen & Unwin, 1957)

Wynmalen, Henry. *Horse Breeding and Stud Management* (Country Life, 1950)

The Arab Horse Society News (Britain), 1955–91

The Arabian – International Magazine (Holland), 1974–76

The Australian Arabian Yearbook, 1989/90, 1990

The Journal of the Arab Horse Society (Britain), 1979

Index

Page numbers in italics refer to illustrations.

Quilty 100 Mile Race, 100

Rabiha, 40, 45
Radi, 29, 30, 36, 48
Rafeef, 36
Rafeena, 31, 82
Raffles, 16, 76
Rafina, 16, 67
Raftan, 39, 120
Rafyk, 66
Ragos, 40, 45
Rajella, 41
Rajmek, 41
Raktha, 30, 31, 81
Raktha Sadha, *83*
Ralvon Elijah, 47, *69*
Ralvon Pilgrim, 70
Ramla, 98
Rangha, 34
Rangoon, 36
Ranya, 38
Ranya II, 31, 38
Raseyn, 75
Rasim, 16, 26, 28, 39
Raswan, Carl (Schmidt), 53, 73–5, 92
Raswan (stallion), 75
Ratcliff, Mrs J., 49
Razalana, 83
Razaz, 70
Razehra, 41, 45
Razina, 28, 29, 30, 31, 81
Razzia, 28
Redif, 38
Reese, H., 75
Rehal, *72*
Rex The Robber, 122
Reyna, 16
Rezah's Tiger Lily, *141*
Riaz, 41
Rice, Fred, *17*
Ridaa, 16
Rifala, 16, 76
Rifari, 36
Riffal, 30, 40, 67
Rifla, 75
Rijm, 26, 36
Rikham, 31, 70
Rikitea, 40, 82
Rim, 16, 73
Risala, 16
Rish, 36
Rishafieh, 84
Rishima, 36

Rishka, 36
Risira, 71
Rissalix, 16, 30, 31, 45
Rissalma, 16
Rissalma (second), 47
Rissam, 30
Rissla, 16, *18*, 36, *37*
Rissletta, 75
Risslina, 16, 36, *37*, 48
Rithan, 45
Rithyana, 42, 45
Riyala, 16, 28
Rizanna, *97*
Roberts, Mrs M., 45
Roda, 73
Rodan, 73
Rodania, 12, 16, 66
Rokhsa, 73
Rosalina, 34
Rosa Rugosa, 25
Rose of France, 76
Rose of Jerico, 66
Rose of Luzon, 76
Rose of Sharon, 16, 66, 72
Rosinella, 67
Rossana, 75
Roxan, *38*, 48
Roxana, 38, 48
Royal Agricultural Society of Egypt (RAS; *see* EAO)
Royal Destiny, 48
Royal Domino, 70
Royal mares, 24
Royal Radiance, 67, 70
Rushcreek Lad, 98
Ruskov, 38
Russell, Miss Mary, 36, 48
Ruth Kesia, 25, 36
Rutland, Duchess of, 48
Rutland Stud, 48
Ruxton, George, 34
Rythma, 16
Rzewuski, Count Waclaw, 56

Saalegrund Stud, 53
Sabek, 47
Safarjal, 19, 26
Sahara, 57
Sahara Ace, *99*
Sahban, 36
Sahirah of the Storm, 42
Sainfoin, 26, 125
Saklavia, 52
Sala, 70

Saladin II, 39
Salome, 71
Salon, 80
Samaveda, 45
Samsie, 30
Sanguszko, Count Eustachy-Erazm, 56
Sanguszko, Prince Hieronymus, 56
Sanguszko, Prince Jerome, 56
Sanguszko, Prince Roman the Elder, 56, 57
Savile, Hon. George, 39
Scherazade, 67, 70
Schmidt, Carl (*see* Raswan)
Scindia, 45
Scindian Enchantress, 103
Scindian Magic, 45, 103
Selby, Roger, 76–7
Selfra, 76
Selima, 16, *17*
Selma, 15, 17
Selmian, 76
Selmnab, 76
Senga, 45
Serafix, 16, 30, *78*
Seyal, 19
Shafreyn, 67
Shagya, 54, 110–12
Shahwan, 19
Shahzada, 25, 36, 67, *123*
Shaker el Masri, 45, 53
Shalawi, 100
Shammar, 27
Shammar, 31
Shareer, 17
Shark, 65
Sherbatov, Prince, 61
Sherifa, 28
Sherifa (Jordan Stud), *iv*
Sheroule, *87*
Sheykh Obeyd Stud, 8, 12, 15, 19
Shihab, 36
Shireen Lailee, *101*
Siglavy, 112
Siglavy Bagdady, 58
Siglavy-Bagdady I, 55
Silent Wings, 17, 103
Silfina, 70
Silvena, *141*
Silver Blue, 47
Silver Circlet, 48
Silver Crystal, 36, 39

149